THE GREAT FINANCIAL CRISIS

CAUSES AND CONSEQUENCES

JOHN BELLAMY FOSTER AND FRED MAGDOFF

Advance Praise for
The Great Financial Crisis

"Everyone at last knows we are in a great financial crisis. Foster and Magdoff have seen it coming for some time now. If you want a clear and cogent explanation of the reality of our debt crisis and what might be done about it, this is your book." —IMMANUEL WALLERSTEIN, Yale University

"*The Great Financial Crisis* will be extremely useful for all who are trying to sort out the meaning of the most serious crisis U.S. and global capitalism has faced in eighty years. Few today are able both to make sense of the details of the modern 'financial architecture' that turned a predictable burst in the U.S. housing bubble into a full scale financial meltdown, and also to bring an historical perspective stemming from the work of Keynes, Hansen, Steindl, Kalecki, Minsky, Galbraith, and of course Marx, Sweezy and Harry Magdoff. Because the authors could draw on their own excellent coverage of the lead up to the crisis in the pages of *Monthly Review* magazine, we have an invaluable book available to us much sooner than would otherwise be possible." — ROBIN HAHNEL, Professor of Economics, American University

"Those of us who are dissatisfied with the analyses of the financial-economic melt-down of 2008 that attribute it to easily remediable 'mistakes' on the part of financial institutions, regulators, or policy-makers can learn a lot from John Bellamy Foster and Fred Magdoff's *The Great Financial Crisis: Causes and Consequences*. Foster and Magdoff follow up the theses of Paul Sweezy, Paul Baran, and Harry Magdoff that diagnose the structural problems of U.S. capitalism in its chronic tendency toward stagnation rooted in inadequate business investment and leading to slow growth, unemployment of labor, and low utilization of capital. This book makes the case that the excesses of financialization and the widening inequality of income distribution are themselves indirect effects of stagnation in the real economy, and explains with sobering clarity why the roots of this crisis may turn out to be deep and difficult to address with conventional policy measures." —DUNCAN K. FOLEY, Leo Model Professor of Economics, New School for Social Research

"Much of the analysis of the latest economic meltdown has been confined to explanations about the housing bubble and bust. In *The Great Financial Crisis*, Foster and Magdoff take a broader approach, presenting a rigorous and sorely needed historical and forward-looking perspective of the capitalist system out of control. With intricate detail, Foster and Magdoff contextualize the housing debt and speculative bubble within its rightful place at the core of an accelerated period of the financialization of capital, eloquently arguing why a people-first, or socialistic, approach to this crisis is the most logical way to stabilize the general economy." —NOMI PRINS, author of *Other People's Money* and *Jacked*

"Harry Magdoff and Paul Sweezy, to whom this book is dedicated, analyzed financial-ization as inseparable from the *tendency to stagnation* of monopoly capital. The present book is written in the same spirit and brings their approach fully up to date under the circumstances of 'monopoly-finance capital.' It underlines that, whatever might be attempted today, the necessarily recurring crisis is bound to get worse without reme-dying the causes of stagnation. Thus Foster and Fred Magdoff rightly stress that 'the answer lies in a truly revolutionary reconstruction of the entire society.' Their book is a worthy memorial to Harry Magdoff and Paul Sweezy." —ISTVÁN MÉSZÁROS, author of *The Challenge and Burden of Historical Time* and *Beyond Capital*

"Foster and Magdoff's very readable account of the crisis merits close and wide atten-tion. Their analysis of consumer debt burdens is the perfect antidote for everyone who is tired of hearing how 'we' went on a consumption binge, and their historically sen-sitive discussions of the roots of the crisis are fresh and provocative." —THOMAS FERGUSON, University of Massachusetts, Boston, author of *The Golden Rule: The Investment Theory of Party Competition and the Logic of Money-Driven Political Systems*

"John Bellamy Foster and Fred Magdoff's book on 'The Great Financial Crisis' is an excellent example of the usefulness of studying Marx's works and that of other Marxist political economists, e.g. the writings of Paul M. Sweezy and Harry Magdoff, in order to better grasp the dynamics and contradictions of the financial turmoil and its implications for social conflict. The disastrous contemporary financial crisis can-not be understood as the consequence of a 'wrong regulation' of the world of finance. It is an emanation of the 'real' accumulation process of financialized monopoly capi-tal." —ELMAR ALTVATER, Otto-Suhr-Institute of the Free University of Berlin

"Foster and Magdoff's new book presents a sharp and stimulating analysis of the his-torical origins and structural roots of the current financial crisis. The authors argue that the implosion is a logical consequence of the contradictions of monopoly finance capital—contradictions that are reflected in the twin processes of financialization and stagnation that have dominated the development of the U.S. economy in the recent decades. It is an essential read if the *mea culpas* and post mortems of 'the experts' faced suddenly with 'a fundamental flaw' in the logic of unregulated markets have left you demanding a more penetrating account of this crisis." —RAMAA VASUDEVAN, Assistant Professor of Economics, Colorado State University

"A must read! Here is an excellent guide to understanding the role debt overload and the stagnation of the real economy played in the recent crisis, in the tradition of Sweezy and Magdoff." —MICHAEL PERELMAN, Professor of Economics, California State University at Chico and author of *Railroading Economics*, *The Invention of Capitalism*, and *The Confiscation of American Prosperity*.

"The financial crisis of 2007-08, and with more certainly in store for 2009 and beyond, is one of the great calamities of modern neoliberal capitalism. But it should come as no surprise for regular readers of John Bellamy Foster and Fred Magdoff's writings over the past few years in *Monthly Review*. In a series of highly accessible and cogent articles, they have consistently explained both the build up to the crisis and its consequences. *The Great Financial Crisis* brings their ideas together in one place. It is compelling reading for anyone seeking to both understand and change the world we live in today." —ROBERT POLLIN, Professor of Economics and Co-Director, Political Economy Research Institute, University of Massachusetts-Amherst.

THE GREAT FINANCIAL CRISIS

Causes and Consequences

John Bellamy Foster and Fred Magdoff

MONTHLY REVIEW PRESS
New York

Library of Congress Cataloging-in-Publication Data
Foster, John Bellamy.
  The great financial crisis : causes and consequences / John Bellamy Foster
and Fred Magdoff.
      p. cm.
  Includes bibliographical references and index.
  1. Financial crises. 2. Debt. 3. Monopolies. 4. Capitalism. I.
Magdoff, Fred, 1942- II. Title.
  HB3722.F66 2009
  330.9'0511--dc22

                        2008044449

ISBN: 978-1-58367-184-9 paper
ISBN: 978-1-58367-185-6 cloth

Monthly Review Press
146 West 29th Street, Suite 6W
New York, NY 10001

5 4 3

CONTENTS

Preface

November 6, 2008

In the profusion of commentaries on the reversals of the U.S. and world economies written over the last few months, perhaps none was more pertinent than the report issued by the U.S. satirical magazine *The Onion* on July 14, 2008, headlined: "Recession-Plagued Nation Demands New Bubble to Invest In." As *The Onion* playfully told its readers, "the U.S. economy cannot survive on sound investments alone. . . . Demand for a new investment bubble began months ago when the subprime mortgage bubble burst and left the business world without a suitable source of pretend income. But as more and more time has passed with no substitute bubble forthcoming, investors have begun to fear that the worst-case scenario—an outcome known among economists as 'real-world repercussions'—may be inevitable." Mockingly raising the question of whether the economy would sink without another financial bubble, *The Onion* cited a make-believe investor: "'America needs another bubble,' said Chicago investor Bob Taiken, 'At this point, bubbles are the only thing keeping us afloat.'" [1] Indeed, in its own ironic way *The Onion* hit on the crucial problem of modern monopoly-finance capital—the stagnation of production and the growth of financial bubbles in response, the bursting of which takes us back to where we began: *real-world repercussions*. This is the story told in this book.

The names with which we choose to represent climactic world-historical events are important. The Great Depression of the 1930s, as distinguished from most other economic disruptions in the history of capitalism, has never ceased to be written in capital letters. Today, in the midst of the worst financial crisis (and leading perhaps to the worst economic crisis generally) since the Great Depression, some have already referred to this as the "Great Financial Crisis."[2] Like the 1929 Stock Market Crash and the Great Depression eighty years ago it represents a turning point in economic history, the full ramifications of which are not yet clear—and indeed depend on the concrete actions people take in response to the crisis. Our purpose here is to examine the causes and consequences of the present Great Financial Crisis, and the radical changes in society that might be undertaken in response—if the great mass of the population decide that economics is really *political* economy and hence theirs to choose.

Even more than most works this book is a case of "standing on the shoulders of giants" who were themselves standing on the shoulders of giants. It is built, as we explain in the following pages, on a foundation laid by Paul Baran, Paul Sweezy, and Harry Magdoff, who in turn relied in various ways on the prior work of Marx, Veblen, Schumpeter, Keynes, Kalecki, Steindl, and Minsky. We do not therefore claim any particular originality for ourselves in this work. Rather it is a continuation and application to current historical developments of an analysis that has evolved over many years, and constitutes an attempt to use this to help ordinary people understand the need for radical change through mass action. We hope that some of those who find this analysis of the Great Financial Crisis useful will be encouraged to seek the longer and deeper analysis of these developments in Baran, Sweezy, and Magdoff . . . all the way back to Marx.

The core of *The Great Financial Crisis* was published first in *Monthly Review* and reflects many years of collaboration in the magazine, which has sought since 1949 to keep an independent socialist voice and a critical perspective alive within the United States. All of those who have been part of this project over the years, including many *MR* readers too numerous to mention, therefore contributed to the formation of these ideas. We would like to thank directly though our closest comrades who have helped us with this book: especially Brett Clark, John Mage, Robert W. McChesney, Claude Misukiewicz, Martin Paddio, John J. Simon, and Michael Yates; and scarcely less importantly Scott Borchert, Yoshie Furuhashi, Hannah Holleman, Ryan Jonna, and Victor Wallis. Carrie Ann Naumoff and Amy Demarest were there with their help and example every step of the way. We dedicate the book itself with fondest memories to Harry and Paul.

Introduction

History is a record of "effects" the vast majority of which
nobody intended to produce.
—Joseph Schumpeter (1939)[1]

The Great Financial Crisis began somewhat inconspicuously in late summer 2007 with the failure of two Bear Stearns hedge funds, and then went from bad to worse over the following year despite countless attempts by governments to halt its progress. It is now universally recognized as the worst economic crash since the Great Depression. Indeed, as U.S. economist and *New York Times* columnist Paul Krugman indicated in late 2008, it raises "the prospect of a second Great Depression."[2]

Although former Federal Reserve Board chairman Alan Greenspan has likened it to "a once-in-a-century credit tsunami," the Great Financial Crisis is a historical rather than natural phenomenon.[3] It represents a development both familiar in the history of capitalism and in many ways historically unprecedented. It was preceded by a whole series of lesser economic shocks, of growing magnitude, over the last two decades, most notably: the U.S. stock market crash of 1987, the savings and loan crisis of the late 1980s and early '90s, the Japanese financial crisis and Great Stagnation of the 1990s, the Asian financial crisis of 1997–1998, and the New Economy (dot-com) crash of 2000. Yet the Great Financial Crisis has far outreached them all. Both the U.S. economy and the economy of the world as a whole are in a state of deep decline, facing what is likely to be a prolonged stagnation. Why is this happening? Are there reasonable grounds to hope that the new administration in Washington with the election of Barack Obama will be able to reverse the course of the economic decline?

For meaningful answers to these questions it is necessary to have a historical perspective going back to the 1930s. Already at the time of the Great Depression John Maynard Keynes, the foremost economist of the twentieth century, argued that capitalism might return to growth and profitability without a return to full employment. As John Kenneth Galbraith stated in *The Age of Uncertainty*:

> Keynes's basic conclusion can . . . be put very directly. Previously it had been held that the economic system, any capitalist system, found its equilibrium at full employment. Left to itself, it was thus that it came to rest. Keynes showed that the modern economy could as well find its equilibrium with continuing, serious underemployment. Its perfectly normal tendency was to what economists have since come to call an underemployment equilibrium.[4]

It was this framework that induced Keynes's leading U.S. follower, Alvin Hansen, to raise the question in 1938 of *Full Recovery or Stagnation?* (in a book with that title). Capitalism, in this view, did not inherently follow a path of full employment and rapid growth, but could be stuck for decades, even permanently, in a condition of slow growth, high unemployment/underemployment, and excess capacity—or stagnation.[5]

In his 1936 classic, *The General Theory of Employment, Interest and Money*—and in other works written at the time of the Depression— Keynes raised the question of a number of flaws internal to the accumulation (savings-and-investment) process under capitalism. His most crucial arguments related to factors leading to a slowdown in investment. For a capitalist economy to work well the surplus (or savings) that it generates must be invested in new productive capacity. Yet, investment in modern capitalism, Keynes argued, was at best a risky undertaking since investment decisions that determine the level of output in the present are based on expectations of profits on this investment a number of years—perhaps as much as a decade—in the future. Under these circumstances, dominated by uncertainty, investment shortfalls can result from any number of factors—including the building up of overcapacity in plant and equipment, a sense that the market for consumer goods is or will soon be saturated, a perception that the external frontier for expansion is limited, etc. High levels of inequality holding down the relative purchasing power of the working class can weaken consumption and hence the expected profits on new investment. Any lessening of investment tends to generate a vicious circle, pulling down employment, income, and spending, generating growing financial problems, and negatively affecting the business climate generally—resulting in an economic slowdown and further investment decline.[6]

It was this analysis of internal contradiction of the capitalist investment process that most strongly influenced the early, more critical Keynesian analyses. The reception of Keynes's *General Theory* in the United States was strongly affected by the recession of 1937, when the U.S. economy experienced a sharp downturn, with unemployment suddenly rising from 14 to 19 percent—far short of a full recovery from the Depression. With around 20 percent of the workforce unemployed nearly a decade after the 1929 stock market crash, economists were faced with the specter of continuing economic stagnation. Departing from the timeless, mechanical models that dominated orthodox economics, Hansen emphasized the long-term implications of Keynes's thinking, presenting what was called the "stagnation thesis."

Hansen focused on the specific historical forces that had propelled the capitalist economy, allowing it to reach a high rate of growth for a period. As *historical* forces these were transitory and waned over time. Moreover, a tendency to "secular stagnation" could be attributed in part to the emergence of "maturity" in capitalist economies. The main components of industry had been built up from scratch in the early phases of industrialization. Investment therefore became increasingly geared to mere replacement (albeit with more efficient plant and equipment) with little new net investment. The result was what Joseph Schumpeter, in a polemic against Hansen, characterized as a theory of "vanishing investment opportunities" (a term Hansen himself accepted). In a 1954 review of Josef Steindl's *Maturity and Stagnation in American Capitalism,* Hansen wrote that "unless fairly drastic action is taken, there is a serious danger that we may move sidewise in the United States or even slip down gradually over the next few years. Measured against the attainable growth of GNP of which we are capable, such an experience would indeed be a form of stagnation."[7]

The Polish Marxist economist Michal Kalecki—often characterized as the most important thinker associated with the "Keynesian Revolution" after Keynes, who had developed the main breakthroughs even before Keynes himself—summed up the essential problem succinctly: "Our analysis shows…that long-run development is not inherent in the capital-ist economy. Thus specific 'development factors' are required to sustain a long-run upward movement."[8]

During the prosperous years of the 1950s and '60s—later referred to as the "Golden Age" of the post–Second World War economy—concerns about stagnation largely disappeared from establishment economics. Keynes's discoveries were tamed and reinserted into the pre-Keynesian neoclassical analysis, producing what came to be known as the "neoclassi-cal-Keynesian synthesis" (dubbed "bastard Keynesianism" by Keynes's younger colleague Joan Robinson).[9] Such was the confidence of ortho-dox economists in this period that Paul Samuelson, a leading figure in the neoclassical-Keynesian synthesis, wrote in 1964 that "the ghost of Thomas Carlyle should be relieved to know that economics, after all, has not been a dismal science. It has been the cheerful, but impatient science of growth."[10] Yet, some radical Keynesian and Marxist economists, defy-ing the dominant view of the times, continued to raise the question of stagnation, arguing that it remained the core problem of the monopoly-capitalist economy and that the prosperity of the 1960s was dependent on short-term stimuli that could not be sustained.

The best known work to make this argument explicitly in the 1960s was Paul Baran and Paul Sweezy's 1966 book, *Monopoly Capital*, which argued that "the *normal* state of the monopoly capitalist economy is stag-nation."[11] Baran and Sweezy were Marxist economists (Sweezy a former professor of economics at Harvard, Baran a professor of economics at Stanford). Both were strongly influenced by Keynes and even more by Kalecki (as well as Marx, Veblen, and Schumpeter). The problem, as they explained it, was that the enormous productivity of the monopoly-capitalist economy, coupled with oligopolistic pricing, generated a huge and growing surplus, which went beyond the capacity of the economy to absorb it through the normal channels of consumption and invest-ment.[12] Effective demand remained insufficient even when civilian gov-ernment spending—which was politically constrained under monopoly capital because of opposition to its intrusion in the sphere of private profits—was added in. The system therefore became dependent on the generation of larger and larger amounts of waste in the form of military spending, the expansion of the sales effort, speculative finance, etc., which functioned as external stimulants boosting production. All of these stimulants, however, were bound to prove inadequate to support the economy over time, since bigger and bigger injections were needed just to keep it going.[13]

Within a few years of their book's publication a renewed crisis set in and the growth rates of the U.S. and other advanced capitalist economies slowed, leading to a dramatic departure from the growth rates of the 1950s and '60s. The "golden age" prosperity turned first, in the colorful language of Joan Robinson, into a "limping golden age" and then into a "leaden age." This slowdown or stagnation has now persisted for four decades, and has only gotten worse over time. "At each recovery from a mild recession," as Robinson wrote of the stagnation exhibited by U.S. capitalism, "the gap between the best realized performance and the potential grows larger."[14]

If the problem of investment as articulated by thinkers like Keynes, Kalecki, Hansen, Baran, Sweezy, and Robinson led to the development of stagnation theory, there was also a second major aspect of Keynes's cri-tique of investment that had closely related adverse implications for the future of capital accumulation, but that was scarcely perceived, even by critical economic thinkers, before the 1970s. This had to do with the con-tradictory role of finance in a capitalist economy, which Keynes had raised in responding to the 1929 stock market crash.[15] The development of the modern corporation was inseparable from the development of modern finance, including the market for industrial securities and the enhanced role given to credit-debt throughout the economy. The stock market itself, Keynes suggested, was primarily a product of the attempts of investors to reduce their risks associated with investment in production through the holding of paper claims to wealth that were more easily transferable. But once this happened, capitalism increasingly took on a dual aspect, reflected in two different pricing structures: the pricing of physical output and the pricing of financial assets. Each operated separately. If long-term assets of corporations were turned into short-term financial commitments for investors the possibility arose, Keynes argued, that the economy would be hostage more and more to speculation over the paper claims to wealth, generating high volatility and instability. As he put it during the early years of the Great Depression,

> There is a multitude of real assets in the world which constitute our capital wealth—buildings, stocks of commodities, goods in course of manufacture and of transport, and so forth. The nominal owners of these assets, however, have not infrequently borrowed *money* in order to become possessed of them. To a corresponding extent the actual owners of wealth have claims, not on real assets, but on money. A considerable part of this "financing" takes place through the banking system, which interposes its guarantee between its depositors who lend it money, and its borrowing customers to whom it loans money wherewith to finance the purchase of real assets. The interposition of this veil of money between the real asset and the wealth owner is a specially marked characteristic of the modern world.[16]

For Keynes, the structure of modern finance invited a periodic decoupling of the market for assets from production—and the possibility that speculative bubbles followed by their inevitable bursting could destabilize the whole system. All of this was made worse as a result of the veil of money and the fact that the banking system tended to be dragged into the center of the maelstrom. As he said in a now frequently quoted passage from *The General Theory*, "Speculators may do no harm as bubbles on a steady stream of enterprise. But the position is serious when enterprise becomes the bubble on a whirlpool of speculation."[17]

Credit for the rediscovery and development of Keynes's insights on finance goes mainly to Hyman Minsky, longtime professor of economics at Washington University (St. Louis), who developed a "financial instability hypothesis" beginning in the 1960s. Minsky was a socialist-oriented economist who had been deeply influenced by the work of Keynes, Kalecki, and Hansen. His financial instability hypothesis argued that the financial structure of the advanced capitalist economy exhibits an internal flaw driving it relentlessly from robustness to fragility, making the whole economy susceptible in the end to debt-deflations of the kind exhibited in the Great Depression. For Minsky the Achilles' heel of a developed financial system was that it was dependent on a constant cash flow of income, in particular profits, to support and "validate" its continued expansion. Over time the instability of the financial system increased, with debt piled on debt in a bubble only waiting to burst when the infusion of cash from income inevitably slowed. The modern economy therefore became chronically dependent on the lender of last resort function of government headquartered in the central banks and treasury departments of the major states, which were charged with propping up the financial structure and avoiding a major debt-deflation by supplying liquidity in a crisis. This in turn required big government, able through the scale of its own economic involvement to stave off a financial crisis by large monetary infusions, acting as lender of last resort.

Minsky's conclusion was stark: "Capitalism is a flawed system in that, if its development is not constrained, it will lead to periodic deep depressions and the perpetuation of poverty." Capitalism, he claimed, did not *necessarily* lead to deep depressions, but there was a continuing race between the increasing scale and fragility of the financial system and the growth of the lender of last resort function. A major concern was that the government as lender of last resort would not be able to keep up with ballooning financial markets unless some restraints were imposed on the latter. The very nature of speculative growth, however, demanded the removal of all such restraints at every sign of crisis if the bubble were not to burst.[18]

Besides Minsky, other dissident economists also focused on the financial instability of capitalism. By far the most persistent and penetrating thinkers in this respect, from the 1960s to the 1990s, were Harry Magdoff and Sweezy, who stressed in one article after another the interrelationship between stagnation and what later came to be known as "financialization" (the shift in gravity of the economy from production to finance). Magdoff, a former New Deal economist at one time responsible for overseeing the publication of the Bureau of Economic Analysis's monthly *Survey of Current Business*, raised the issue as early as 1965 of the long-term increase in debt in relation to the underlying economy, as a possible destabilizing trend.[19] In the following decades Magdoff and Sweezy, writing in *Monthly Review*, tracked this aspect of monopoly capitalism empirically year after year, and sometimes even month by month.

What was missing from Minsky's financial instability theory, Magdoff and Sweezy argued, was the explicit recognition of reemerging stagnation, already evident by the mid-1960s and gaining strength in the 1970s. This set the conditions for a major change in the role of the financial sector in U.S. capitalism. Rather than being a modest helper to the capital accumulation process, it gradually turned into a driving force. Speculative finance became a kind of secondary engine for growth given the weakness in the primary engine, productive investment. The result was an acceleration of the process of debt buildup—going beyond mere speculative orgies that historically came at the peak of business cycles, becoming instead a permanent, institutionalized feature of the economy. The search by capital for profitable outlets for its surplus despite the stagnation of investment opportunities within production, coupled with the belief that asset prices as a whole went only one way—up—generated a secular financial explosion. The system became more and more dependent on a series of financial bubbles to keep it going, each one bigger than the last. The specter of a major devaluation of capital loomed ever larger as a result of these developments, while the financial explosion (together with other stimuli such as military spending, the sales effort, etc.) was, despite its stratospheric rise, unable to prevent a process of creeping stagnation from taking over.

For Magdoff and Sweezy, the essence of capitalism's dilemma in its monopoly stage was captured by the "symbiotic embrace" that had emerged between stagnation and financialization. The economy could not live without financialization (along with other props to the system such as military spending) and it could not in the end live with it.[20]

Our argument in this book, derived from Magdoff and Sweezy in particular, is that a realistic assessment of recent economic history is best conducted within a framework that focuses on the interrelationship between the stagnation tendency of monopoly capital and the forces that to some extent counter it. The largest of the countervailing forces during the last three decades is financialization—so much so that we can speak today of "monopoly-finance capital." The expansion of debt and speculation that characterized the U.S. economy (and advanced capitalism as a whole) since the late 1960s represented the main means by which the system managed to avoid sinking into a deep slump, while not enabling it to overcome the underlying stagnation tendency. Hence, it is in this complex dynamic that answers to the present economic predicament are to be found. This is illustrated in Chart I showing, by means of a time series index (1959 = 100), a decline in the rate of goods production as a percentage of GDP in the economy, and a rise at the same time of debt as a percentage of GDP. Not only do the changes in debt and goods production as percentages of GDP head off in opposite directions, but the gap rapidly widens.

Two things should be underscored here. First, financialization, manifested in the growth of debt relative to GDP, has been a *long-term trend* that accelerated beginning in the 1980s. The debt overhang in this period is therefore not simply a short-lived phenomenon occurring at the end of a business cycle peak, as in the case of most speculative booms historically. Second, the stagnation of goods production relative to GDP has worsened over time, despite the enormous economic lift provided by the financial explosion.

There is a temptation of some analysts, particularly on the left, to see finance as simply a parasitic phenomenon—and that all could be put right simply by rechanneling these funds to productive investment.[21] However, the argument presented in this book, as the foregoing sug-

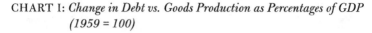

CHART I: *Change in Debt vs. Goods Production as Percentages of GDP (1959 = 100)*

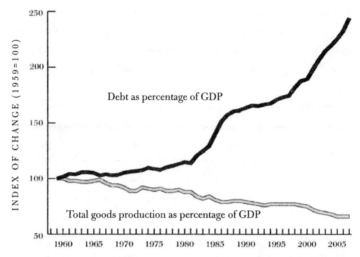

Sources: Calculated from Federal Reserve, Flow of Funds Accounts of the United States, "Credit Market Debt Outstanding," Table L.1; *Economic Report of the President, 2008*, "Gross Domestic Product, 1959–2007," Table B-1 and "Gross Domestic Product by major type of product, 1959–2007," Table B-8.

gests, is different. The financial explosion in the U.S. and other advanced capitalist economies since the 1960s, we argue, is symptomatic of the underlying stagnation tendency that has its roots in the whole pattern of accumulation under monopoly-finance capital. It is this and not the financialization (or even today's crisis of financialization) that is the real problem.

Marx explained that capital was invariably overextended in a boom and that in the crisis that followed a part of this capital was devalued, enabling the rest to return to profitability and to the process of accumulation and expansion. Crises thus resulted from the "overproduction of capital." Indeed, "The *real barrier* of capitalist production," Marx wrote, "is *capital itself*."[22] The system is now hard up against this barrier in multiple ways. There is no possibility that the enormous surplus capital that has fed the financial explosion can be absorbed by productive investment under the present system at this stage in its history and with the existing structure of inequality. At the same time the financialization process itself is now in crisis. The most likely prospect therefore is a prolonged, deep stagnation.

All of this is necessary background to the story told in this book. In what follows the Great Financial Crisis is addressed chronologically, with the chapters consisting of analyses originally written as parts of a running commentary during the years 2006–2008 as the present crisis took shape. We have purposely kept the first five chapters unchanged, leaving them in the form in which they were originally published (with only minor copy-editing changes), to reflect the concrete application of the stagnation-financialization perspective to the crisis at each stage of its development.[23] The sixth chapter (along with this introduction) was written especially for this book. Part One on historical *causes* proceeds from a consideration of the household debt bubble (Chapter 1), to the wider explosion of debt and speculation (Chapter 2), to the emergence of monopoly-finance capital (Chapter 3), and finally to the larger problem of the financialization of capital (Chapter 4). Part Two on *consequences*—or the actual playing out of the crisis and its long-term implications—begins with the crisis of financialization and the onset of the Great Financial Crisis (Chapter 5), proceeding to a treatment of the full financial implosion as 2009 approached (Chapter 6). We end the final chapter with a consideration of the larger *political*-economic aspects of the crisis.

A self-imposed limitation of our analysis here is its focus almost exclusively on the development of the Global Financial Crisis in the context of the U.S. economy, addressing only tangentially the other advanced capitalist economies, the "emerging" economies, the underdeveloped economies, and the world economy as a whole. We also refrain from examining in any detail the U.S. current account deficit or the role of the dollar as a surrogate world currency.[24] Needless to say, these are all important parts of the overall story. Our decision to impose these limits is based on our conviction that the main contradictions of capitalism are still best perceived, as Marx emphasized in the nineteenth century, from the standpoint of the preeminent capitalist economy at a given stage of its development (in the nineteenth century, Britain, in the twentieth and early twenty-first centuries, the United States). Moreover, the United

States is without a doubt the principal source of the current economic firestorm. Finally, the global ramifications of the Great Financial Crisis need to be understood in the first instance in the context of the waning political, economic, and military hegemony of the United States. We hope that our focus on the U.S. economy shall prove to be a useful contribution to the wider story that still remains to be told.

Ultimately, we believe the Great Financial Crisis raises questions that are primarily political rather than economic. Many naturally hope that the new administration in Washington, with the election of Barack Obama, will provide an opportunity to carry out major changes to overcome this crisis and its worst effects by ushering in a new New Deal.[25] The question thus arises: Is it possible to create a new New Deal on the scale of the late 1930s in Roosevelt's second administration—or to go even further in promoting civilian government spending and progressive social change? As John Kenneth Galbraith wrote in 2004 in his *Economics of Innocent Fraud*, "The one wholly reliable remedy for recession is a solid flow of consumer demand. Failure in such a flow is a recession. In the United States especially with stagnation and recession, the lower income citizen has an acute need for education, health care, a basic family income in one form or another."[26] Would a concerted spending program devoted to these ends bring the crisis to an end?

Our answer to this is complex and in this introduction must be necessarily brief. First, it is essential to note that what pulled the United States out of the Great Depression of the 1930s was not civilian government spending in the New Deal (one out of five workers was still unemployed in 1938) but rather the enormous expansion of military spending with the coming of the Second World War, beginning in 1939. Under the stimulus of wartime demand, the U.S. economy increased in size by 70 percent in only six years. However, with U.S. military expenditures today constituting almost half of total world military spending (U.S. military expenditures in 2007 were officially over $550 billion a year but in reality $1 trillion a year)—all of which is geared to maintaining the greatest empire the world has ever seen—it is obvious that this war machine needs to be drastically cut, not expanded. The way out of the Great

Depression cannot be duplicated without threatening world annihilation. Indeed, any program for social progress emanating in the United States that did not begin by seeking to dismantle the U.S. empire would be a travesty from the start.[27]

Second, given the existing power relations in the United States, any endeavor to replicate the New Deal is unlikely to gain much traction. In the current rules of the game it would be hamstrung from the start by entrenched vested interests. This is not to deny of course that such a new New Deal, if it were carried out in a radical spirit (as represented for example by the Works Progress Administration in the late 1930s), could do much to help the general population in the context of the crisis, reducing some inequities. But it would likely soon succumb to its own and capitalism's contradictions.

Nevertheless, if such a movement for radical reform were actually tried and yet failed (we think inevitably) to remove the injustices and irrationalities of the system, there would be no need to go back to square one. Rather the population would be fully justified in such a case in pushing forward and concluding that the entire political-economic structure should be replaced, brick by brick, with another that would meet their genuine needs and be under their democratic control: a system of social use rather than private gain. Already peoples throughout the world have reached the conclusion that the only rational answer is to replace the current rotten system with a more humane order geared to collective needs. For centuries the friends and enemies of social progress have called this alternative of a people-directed economy and society "socialism." We can think of no better name.

PART ONE

Causes

1. The Household Debt Bubble
May 2006

It is an inescapable truth of the capitalist economy that the uneven, class-based distribution of income is a determining factor of consumption and investment. How much is spent on consumption goods depends on the income of the working class. Workers necessarily spend all or almost all of their income on consumption. Thus for households in the bottom 60 percent of the income distribution in the United States, average personal consumption expenditures equaled or exceeded average pre-tax income in 2003; while the fifth of the population just above them used up five-sixths of their pre-tax income (most of the rest no doubt taken up by taxes) on consumption.[1] In contrast, those high up on the income pyramid—the capitalist class and their relatively well-to-do hangers-on—spend a much smaller percentage of their income on personal consumption. The overwhelming proportion of the income of capitalists (which at this level has to be extended to include unrealized capital gains) is devoted to investment.

It follows that increasing inequality in income and wealth can be expected to create the age-old conundrum of capitalism: an accumulation (savings-and-investment) process that depends on keeping wages down while ultimately relying on wage-based consumption to support economic growth and investment. It is impossible to do as suggested by the early-twentieth-century U.S. economist J. B. Clark—to "build more mills that should make more mills for ever"—in the absence of sufficient consumer demand for the products created by these mills.[2]

Under these circumstances, in which consumption and ultimately investment are heavily dependent on the spending of those at the bottom of the income stream, one would naturally suppose that a stagnation or decline in real wages would generate crisis-tendencies for the economy by constraining overall consumption expenditures. There is no doubt about the growing squeeze on wage-based incomes. Except for a small rise in the late 1990s, real wages have been sluggish for decades. The typical (median-income) family has sought to compensate for this by increasing its number of jobs and working hours per household. Nevertheless, the real (inflation-adjusted) income of the typical household fell for five years in a row through 2004. The bottom 95 percent of income recipients experienced decreasing real average household income in 2003–04 (with the top 5 percent, however, making sharp gains). In 2005 real wages fell by 0.8 percent.[3]

Yet, rather than declining as a result, overall consumption has continued to climb. Indeed, U.S. economic growth is ever more dependent on what appears at first glance to be unstoppable increases in consumption. Between 1994 and 2004 consumption grew faster than national income, with the share of personal consumption expenditures in GDP rising from 67 to 70 percent.[4] How is this paradox—declining real wages and soaring consumption—to be explained?

Commenting on this same problem in May 2000 (near the end of the previous business cycle expansion) the *Monthly Review* editors asked:

> But if this [stagnating wages] is the case, where is all of the consumption coming from? Has capital managed somehow to square the circle—to increase consumption rapidly while simultaneously holding down wages? The obvious answer—or a good part of it—is that in a period of stagnant wages, working people are increasingly living beyond their means by borrowing in order to make ends meet (or, in some cases, in a desperate attempt to inch up their living standards). To a considerable extent, the current economic expansion has been bought on consumer debt.

If this was the case six years ago just before the last economic downturn, it is even more so today and the potential consequences are worse. Since consumption expenditures have been rising in the United States much faster than income the result has been a rise in the ratio of overall consumer debt to disposable income. As shown in Table 1.1, the ratio of outstanding consumer debt to consumer disposable income has more than doubled over the last three decades from 62 percent in 1975 to 127 percent in 2005. This is partly made possible by historically low interest rates, which have made it easier to service the debt in recent years (although interest rates are now rising). Hence, a better indication of the actual financial impact of the debt on households is provided by the debt service ratio—consumer debt service payments to consumer disposable income. Chart 1.1 shows the rapid increase in the debt service ratio during the quarter-century from 1980 to the present, with a sharp upturn beginning in the mid-1990s and continuing with only slight interruptions ever since.

TABLE 1.1: *Outstanding Consumer Debt as a Percentage of Disposable Income (in billions of dollars)*

	Consumer Debt	Consumer Disposable Income	Debt as % of Disposable Income
1975	736.3	1,187.4	62.0
1980	1,397.1	2,009.0	69.5
1985	2,272.5	3,109.3	73.0
1990	3,592.9	4,285.8	83.8
1995	4,858.1	5,408.2	89.8
2000	6,960.6	7,194.0	96.8
2005	11,496.6	9,039.5	127.2

Note: Disposable income after paying taxes

Source: Board of Governors of the Federal Reserve System, Flow of Funds Accounts of the United States, Historical Series and Annual Flows and Outstandings, Fourth Quarter 2005 (March 9, 2006). Available at http://www.federalreserve.gov/releases/Z1/Current/.

Aggregate data of this kind, however, does not tell us much about the impact of such debt on various income groups (classes). For information on that it is necessary to turn to the Federal Reserve Board's Survey of Consumer Finances, which is carried out every three years. Table 1.2

provides data on what is known as the "family debt burden" (debt service payments as a percentage of disposable income) by income percentiles. Although the family debt burden fell for almost all levels of income during the most recent recession (marked by the 2001 survey) it has risen sharply during the latest sluggish expansion. For those families in the median-income percentiles (40.0–59.9), debt burdens have now reached their peak levels for the entire period 1995–2004. These families have seen their debt service payments as a percentage of disposable income increase by about 4 percentage points since 1995, to almost 20 percent—higher than any other income group. The lowest debt burden is natural-

CHART 1.1: *Consumer Debt Service Ratio (Debt Service Payments to Disposable Income)*

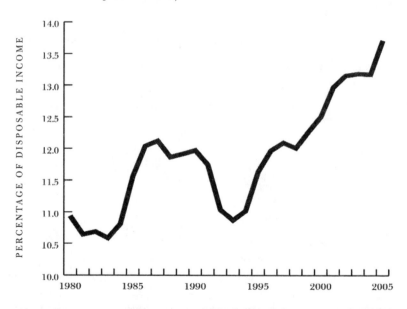

Source: Board of Governors, Federal Reserve Board, Household Debt Service and Financial Obligations Ratios, www.federalreserve.gov/releases/housedebt/

Note: The debt service ratios provided in the Federal Reserve's Household Debt Service and Financial Obligations Ratios data (used in this chart) and in the Survey of Consumer Finances (used in the following tables) are not directly comparable. The data here is based on aggregate consumer debt service to aggregate consumer disposable income and not on survey data as in the tables that follow.

ly to be found in those in the highest (90–100) income percentiles, where it drops to less than 10 percent of disposable income.

TABLE 1.2: *Family Debt Burden. Debt Service Payments as a Percentage of Family Income*

Income Percentile	1995	1998	2001	2004
< 20	19.1	18.7	16.1	18.2
20–39.9	17.0	16.5	15.8	16.7
40–59.9	15.6	18.6	17.1	19.4
60–79.9	17.9	19.1	16.8	18.5
80–89.9	16.6	16.8	17.0	17.3
90–100	9.5	10.3	8.1	9.3

Source: Board of Governors of the Federal Reserve System, "Recent Changes in U.S. Family Finances: Results from the 2001 and 2004 Survey of Consumer Finances,"[5] *Federal Reserve Bulletin* (2006), www.federalreserve.gov/pubs/bulletin/2006/financesurvey.pdf/

All of this points to the class nature of the distribution of household debt. This is even more obvious when one looks at those indebted families who carry exceptionally high debt burdens and those that are more than sixty days past due in their debt service payments. Table 1.3 shows the percentage of indebted families by income percentiles that have family debt burdens above 40 percent. Such financial distress is inversely correlated with income. More than a quarter of the poorest indebted families—those in the lowest fifth of all families—are carrying such heavy debt burdens. The next two-fifths above that, i.e., the 20.0–59.9 income percentiles, have experienced increases in the percentage of indebted families carrying such excessive debt burdens since 1995—with the number of indebted families caught in this debt trap rising to around 19 percent in the second lowest quintile, and to around 14 percent even in the middle quintile. In contrast, for those in the 40 percent of families with the highest incomes, the percentage of households experiencing such financial distress has diminished since 1995. Thus with the rapid rise in outstanding debt to disposable income, financial distress is ever more solidly based in lower-income, working-class families.

TABLE 1.3: *Percentage of Indebted Families Whose Debt Service Payments are Above 40 Percent of Family Income*

Income Percentile	1995	1998	2001	2004
< 20	27.5	29.9	29.3	27.0
20–39.9	18.0	18.3	16.6	18.6
40–59.9	9.9	15.8	12.3	13.7
60–79.9	7.7	9.8	6.5	7.1
80–89.9	4.7	3.5	3.5	2.4
90–100	2.3	2.8	2.0	1.8

Source: See note to Table 1.2.

Soaring family debt burdens naturally pave the way to defaults and bankruptcies. Personal bankruptcies during the first G. W. Bush administration totaled nearly five million, a record for any single term in the White House. Due to the harsh bankruptcy legislation passed by Congress in 2005 the number of bankruptcies has recently declined—at least in the short term. But by making it more difficult for families to free themselves from extreme debt burdens, this is certain to produce ever greater numbers of workers who are essentially "modern-day indentured servants."[6]

Table 1.4 shows the percentage of indebted families in each income category that are sixty days or more past due on any debt service payment. For families below the 80th percentile in income the percentage of indebted families falling into this category has grown sharply since 1995. In contrast, families in the 80th percentile and above have seen a drop in the percentage of indebted families that are overdue on a debt payment. Again, we see that the growth of financial distress in the United States today is centered on working-class households.

The biggest portion of debt is secured by primary residence, the main asset of the vast majority of families. Debt secured by homes has continued to soar. Between 1998 and 2001 the median amount of home-secured debt rose 3.8 percent; while from 2001–04 it rose a phenomenal 27.3 percent! Around 45 percent of homeowners with a first-lien mortgage refinanced

TABLE 1.4: *Percentage of Indebted Families Whose Debt Service Payments Are Sixty Days or More Past Due on Any Debt Service Payment*

Income Percentile	1995	1998	2001	2004
< 20	10.2	12.9	13.4	15.9
20–39.9	10.1	12.3	11.7	13.8
40–59.9	8.7	10.0	7.9	10.4
60–79.9	6.6	5.9	4.0	7.1
80–89.9	2.8	3.9	2.6	2.3
90–100	1.0	1.6	1.3	.3

Source: See note to Table 1.2.

their homes in 2001–04 (as compared with 21 percent in the previous three years), with more than a third of these borrowing money beyond the amount refinanced. The median amount of the additional equity extracted by such borrowers was $20,000.[7] Despite skyrocketing house prices in recent years the ratio of homeowners' equity/value of household real estate has continued to decrease from 68 percent in 1980–89, to 59 percent in 1990–99, to 57 percent in 2000–05.[8]

As house prices have soared more risky forms of mortgage lending have emerged. *Left Business Observer* editor Doug Henwood noted in *The Nation*,

> Time was, you had to come up with a hefty down payment to buy a house. No longer: In 2005 the median first-time buyer put down only 2 percent of the sales price, and 43 percent made no down payment at all. And almost a third of new mortgages in 2004 and '05 were at adjustable rates (because the initial payments are lower than on fixed-rate loans). At earlier peaks interest rates were near cyclical highs, but the past few years have seen the lowest interest rates in a generation. So adjustable mortgages are likely to adjust only one way: up.[9]

The typical family is also mired in credit card debt. At present nearly two-thirds of all cardholders carry balances and pay finance fees each month—with the average debt balance per cardholder rising to $4,956 at the end of 2005. In recent years, there has been a shift from fixed to variable rate cards, as interest rates have begun to rise, with about two-thirds of all credit cards now carrying variable rates—up from a little more than half a year ago. Interest rates on cards are rising rapidly—what the *Wall Street Journal* has called "The Credit-Card Catapult." In February 2006 the average interest rate for variable-rate cards jumped to 15.8 percent from 12.8 percent for all of 2005. Meanwhile, the portion of credit card-issuer profits represented by fees went up from 28 percent in 2000 to an estimated 39 percent in 2004. Altogether, unpaid credit card balances at the end of 2005 amounted to a total of $838 billion.[10] The effects of this fall most heavily on working-class and middle-income families. According to the Survey of Consumer Finances, the percentage of households carrying credit card balances rises with income up until the 90th income percentile, and then drops precipitously.

Another realm of increased borrowing is installment borrowing, encompassing loans that have fixed payments and fixed terms such as automobile loans and student loans—constituting the two biggest areas of installment borrowing. In 2001–04 the average amount owed on such loans grew by 18.2 percent.[11]

Low-income families are more and more subject to predatory lending: payday loans, car title loans, subprime mortgage lending, etc.—all of which are growing rapidly in the current climate of financial distress. According to the Center for Responsible Lending,

> A typical car title loan has a triple-digit annual interest rate, requires repayment within one month, and is made for much less than the value of the car. . . . Because the loans are structured to be repaid as a single balloon payment after a very short term, borrowers frequently cannot pay the full amount due on the maturity date and instead find themselves extending or "rolling over" the loan repeatedly. In this way, many borrowers pay fees well in excess of the amount they originally borrowed. If the borrower fails to keep up with these recurring payments, the lender may summarily repossess the car.[12]

The growing financial distress of households has led to the rise of an army of debt collectors, with the number of companies specializing in buying and collecting unpaid debts rising from around 12 in 1996 to more than 500 by 2005. According to the *Washington Post*, this has led to: "Embarrassing calls at work. Threats of jail and even violence. Improper withdrawals from bank accounts. An increasing number of consumers are complaining of abusive techniques from companies that are a new breed of debt collectors."[13]

In this general context of rising household debt, it is of course the rapid increase in home-secured borrowing that is of the greatest macroeconomic significance, and that has allowed this system of debt expansion to balloon so rapidly. Homeowners are increasingly withdrawing equity from their homes to meet their spending needs and pay off credit card balances. As a result, "in the October to December [2005] period, the volume of new net home mortgage borrowing rose by $1.11 trillion, bringing the level of outstanding mortgage debt to $8.66 trillion—an amount that equaled 69.4 percent of U.S. GDP."[14] The fact that this is happening at a time of growing inequality of income and wealth and stagnant or declining real wages and real income for most people leaves little doubt that it is driven to a considerable extent by need as families try to maintain their living standards.

The housing bubble, associated with rising house prices and the attendant increases in home refinancing and spending, which has been developing for decades, was a major factor in allowing the economy to recover from the 2000 stock market meltdown and the recession in the following year. Only two years after the stock market decline, the iconoclastic economist and financial analyst Stephanie Pomboy of MacroMavens was writing of "The Great Bubble Transfer," in which the continuing expansion of the housing bubble was miraculously compensating for the decline in the stock market bubble by spurring growth in its stead. Yet, "like the bubble in financial assets," Pomboy wrote,

> The new real estate bubble has its own distinctly disturbing characteristics. For example one could argue, and quite cogently, that the home has become the new "margin account" as consumers through popular programs like "cash-out" Refi[nancing] increasingly leverage against unrealized gains in their single largest asset. Perhaps the most disturbing hall-

mark of this Refi mania is the corresponding plunge in homeowners' equity-stake.... The cash-out Refi numbers reveal a "speculative fervor" that makes the Nasdaq mania look tame. According to estimates by Fannie Mae, the average cash-out Refi is $34,000. This sounds like a lot to me, particularly considering that the median home price is just $150,000 ... e.g., the average Joe is extracting 20% of his home value![15]

The surprising strength of consumption expenditures, rising faster than disposable income, has most often been attributed to the stock market wealth effect (the notion that the equivalent of a couple of percentages of increases in stock market wealth go to enhanced consumption expenditures by the rich—those who mostly own the nation's stocks).[16] Pomboy argues, however, that "there is evidence to suggest that the housing wealth effect may be significantly larger than the stock market wealth effect.... Based on a recent study by Robert Shiller (of 'Irrational Exuberance' fame) housing has *always* been a more important driver for consumers than the stock market. In his rigorous state by state and 14 country analysis, he found housing to have *twice* the correlation with consumption than the stock market has." For Pomboy, this suggested that the writing was on the wall: "With homeowners' equity near all-time lows, any softening in home prices could engender the risk of a cascade into negative equity. But even more immediately, the increase in mortgage debt service (again, despite new lows in mortgage rates) does not bode well for consumption as the Fed prepares to reverse course"—and raise interest rates.

The decrease in home equity and the increase in mortgage debt service (and the debt service ratio as a whole) suggest how great the "speculative fervor" underpinning consumption growth actually is today. The housing bubble and the strength of consumption in the economy are connected to what might be termed the "household debt bubble," which could easily burst as a result of rising interest rates and the stagnation or decline of housing prices. Indeed, the median price of a new home has declined for four straight months at the time of this writing, with sales of new single-family homes dropping by 10.5 percent in February, the biggest decline in almost a decade, possibly signaling a bursting of the housing bubble.

In a recent interview, "Handling the Truth," in *Barron's* magazine, Stephanie Pomboy argued that the U.S. economy was headed into "an environment of stagflation [tepid growth combined with high unemployment and rising prices]." Among the reasons for this, she claimed, were the weaknesses in wage income and the inability of consumers to continue to support the household debt bubble. "Already, consumer purchasing power is limited by . . . lackluster income growth, specifically wages." For Pomboy, corporations have been increasingly focusing on the high end of the consumer market in recent years, while the low end (that part supported by wage-based consumers) is in danger of collapsing. Even Wal-Mart, the bastion of low prices that caters primarily to the working class, is beginning to stock products that they hope will attract higher-income families.[17]

The weakness of incomes at the bottom, and the squeeze on working-class consumption—so-called "low-end consumption"—is a serious concern for an economy that has become more and more dependent on consumption to fuel growth, given the stagnation of investment. With declining expectations of profit on new investment, corporations have been sitting on vast undistributed corporate profits, which rose, Pomboy says, as high as $500 billion and are now around $440 billion. The total cash available to corporations, just "sitting in the till," at the end of 2005 was, according to *Barron's*, a record $2 trillion. "The shocking thing, obviously," Pomboy states, "is that they have been sitting on this cash and they are not doing anything with it despite incredible incentives to spend it, not just fiscally but from an interest-rate standpoint. It's not like keeping and sitting on cash is a particularly compelling investment idea right now. It speaks a lot about the environment that CEOs see out there with potentially the continued [capital] overhang that we've got from the post-bubble period."[18]

The truth is that without a step-up in business investment the U.S. economy will stagnate—a reality that speculative bubbles can hold off and disguise in various ways, though not entirely overcome. But investment is blocked by overaccumulation and overcapacity. Hence, the likely result is continued slow growth, the further piling up of debt, and the potential for financial meltdowns. There is no growth miracle whereby a mature capitalist economy prone to high exploitation and vanishing investment opportunities (and unable to expand net exports to the rest of the world) can continue to grow rapidly—other than through the action of bubbles that only threaten to burst in the end.

The tragedy of the U.S. economy is not one of excess consumption but of the ruthless pursuit of wealth by a few at the cost of the population as a whole. In the end the only answer lies in a truly revolutionary reconstruction of the entire society. Such a radical reconstruction is obviously not on the table right now. Still, it is time for a renewed class struggle from below—not only to point the way to an eventual new system, but also, more immediately, to protect workers from the worst failures of the old. There is no question where such a struggle must begin: labor must rise from its ashes.

2. The Explosion of Debt and Speculation
November 2006

STAGNATION AND FINANCE

In a series of articles in *Monthly Review* and in Monthly Review Press books during the 1970s and 1980s, Harry Magdoff and Paul Sweezy proposed that the general economic tendency of mature capitalism is toward stagnation.[1] A shortage of profitable investment opportunities is the primary cause of this tendency. Less investment in the productive economy (the "real economy") means lower future growth. Marx wrote about the possibility of this very phenomenon:

> If this new accumulation meets with difficulties in its employment, through a lack of spheres of investment, i.e. due to a surplus in the branches of production and an over-supply of loan capital, this plethora of loanable money capital merely shows the limitations of *capitalist* production . . . an obstacle is indeed immanent in its laws of expansion, i.e., in the limits in which capital can realise itself as capital.[2]

Stagnation, of course, does not mean that there is no growth whatsoever. Rather, the economy functions well below its potential—with appreciable unused productive capacity and significant unemployment and underemployment. Over the last thirty years an average of 81 percent of industrial capacity was used, and during the last five years the average was only 77 percent. There is normally significant unused production capacity even in the recovery phase of the business cycle. During the largely boom years of the 1960s the manufacturing sector was producing at close to 85 percent of capacity; even in the best year, 1966 (during the Vietnam War), manufacturing production only reached 91 percent of capacity.

With regard to labor utilization, the official rate of unemployment in July 2006 stood at a relatively low 4.8 percent. However, the Bureau of Labor Statistics' "alternate measure of labor utilization"—which includes, in addition to the "officially" unemployed, an assessment of those who have given up looking for work, plus those working part-time but desiring full-time employment—shows that some 8 percent of the potential labor force is underemployed or unemployed. Even this seems to be an understatement given the decrease of labor force participation under the stagnant financially led economy. Despite the category of "marginally attached workers" in the alternate unemployment measure, existing methodologies do not fully capture the portion of those who have ostensibly dropped out of the workforce but who are actually desirous of jobs. In the present period such deep, chronic discouragement forcing potential workers out of the labor pool seems to be continuing despite the business cycle upturn. Labor participation rates have thus declined since 2000—a phenomenon that is almost unprecedented for the post–Second World War period and has given rise to much controversy.[3]

Indeed, the average gain in actual employment since the end of the last recession has been extremely sluggish. As economics writer Floyd Norris pointed out, "At this point after the previous nine recessions, there were an average of 11.9 percent more jobs in the economy than there had been at the end of the recession. But so far [August 2006] . . . there are just 3.5 percent more jobs than at the end of the last recession."[4] Thus, three years into a recovery from a relatively mild recession we still have significant indicators of stagnation.

Capitalist economies are based on the profit motive and accumulation of capital without end. Hence problems arise whenever they do not expand at reasonably high growth rates. Those problems range from high unemployment/underemployment to frequent recessions to stock market crashes to inflation to deflation. A number of mechanisms, which are briefly assessed below, have served either to counterbalance or represent attempts to overcome mature capitalism's tendency toward stagnation. However, as Magdoff and Sweezy pointed out: "The tendency to stagnation is inherent in the system, deeply rooted and in continuous operation. The counter-tendencies, on the other hand, are varied, intermittent, and (most important), self-limiting."[5]

IMPERIALISM, GLOBALIZATION, AND STAGNATION

As industries mature and their products saturate markets at home corporations seeking profitable outlets for their commodities and their capital increasingly attempt to export products and invest abroad. This, together with other important objectives—such as controlling sources of raw materials needed for production and taking advantage of low wages and lax environmental and labor safety standards—augments the imperialist drive that is an essential characteristic of capitalism. Neoliberal globalization is the most recent manifestation of imperialism: capital (large corporations, both financial and non-financial) using governments, and especially the leadership of the U.S. government, to make it easier to exploit the world's resources and people. The ideal situation for capitalists is to be able to invest and sell where and when they want, to move money and products in and out of countries and to repatriate profits at will.

This imperial thrust growing out of the natural workings of a capitalist economy provides profitable outlets that might not be available in the home country as well as enhanced profitability at home, through control of markets for raw materials needed by industries. To give some idea of the importance of profits from investments abroad in the total U.S. economy, these represented about 6 percent of total business profits in the 1960s, 11 percent in the 1970s, 15 to 16 percent in the 1980s and '90s, and have averaged 18 percent for the five-year period 2000–04.[6]

It is true that investment in the periphery has created new outlets for investment-seeking capital. However, for a variety of reasons, such as the worldwide competition for markets, global stagnation (evident in the growth of worldwide excess capacity) and the soaring surplus obtained from exploitation of third world markets, which adds to the capital look-

ing for outlets, such external expansion has not seriously alleviated the
tendency toward an overaccumulation of capital on either a U.S. or
world scale.

KEY INVENTIONS AND TECHNOLOGIES
AS ECONOMIC STIMULI

Key inventions and technologies have at times significantly stimulated the
economy, sometimes for decades. For example, the invention of the automobile in the early twentieth century led eventually to huge developments
that transformed the U.S. economy, even aside from the mass ownership
of automobiles: the building of an extensive system of roads, bridges, and
tunnels; the need for a network of gas stations, restaurants, automotive
parts and repair shops; the efficient and inexpensive movement of goods
from any location to any other location. Another of the profound effects
of the widespread personal use of the automobile was the increase in sub-
urbanization of housing. On the negative side, the automobile virtually
eliminated much urban and interurban public surface transportation, created a vast new source of pollution (and carbon dioxide), and by the second half of the twentieth century compelled U.S. foreign policy to ensure
that oil and gas continued to flow to power such developments.

Thus, the technology of the automobile stimulated the economy for
decades of the twentieth century in numerous ways. The new information
technologies (computers, software, the Internet), while certainly changing the way individuals and companies work, do not appear to be providing a similar epoch-making, long-term economic stimulus, although the
"silicon revolution" has had important economic consequences.

GROWTH OF GOVERNMENT SPENDING
AS A COUNTER TO STAGNATION

Government spending on physical and human infrastructure, as Keynes
pointed out, can also fuel the economy: the interstate highway system, for
instance, bolstered the economy directly by creating jobs and indirectly
by making production and sales more efficient. However, spending on the
military has a special stimulating effect. As Harry Magdoff put it,

A sustainable expanding market economy needs active investment as well as plenty of consumer demand. Now the beauty part of militarism for the vested interests is that it stimulates and supports investment in capital goods as well as research and development of products to create new industries. . . . Military orders made significant and sometimes decisive difference in the shipbuilding, machine tools and other machinery industries, communication equipment, and much more . . . the explosion of war material orders gave aid and comfort to the investment goods industries. (As late as 1985, the military bought 66 percent of aircraft manufactures, 93 percent of shipbuilding, and 50 percent of communication equipment). . . . Spending for the Korean War was a major lever in the rise of Germany and Japan from the rubble. Further boosts to their economies came from U.S. spending abroad for the Vietnamese War.[7]

The rise of the silicon-based industries and the Internet are two relatively recent examples of how military projects "create new industries." Additionally, actual warfare such as the U.S. wars against Iraq and Afghanistan (and the supplying of Israel to carry out its most recent war in Lebanon) stimulates the economy by requiring the replacement of equipment that wears out rapidly under battle conditions as well as the spent missiles, bullets, bombs, etc.

To get an idea of how important military expenditures are to the United States economy, let's look at how they stack up against expenditures for investment purposes. The category gross private investment includes all investment in business structures (factories, stores, power stations, etc.), business equipment and software, and home/apartment construction. This investment creates both current and future growth in the economy as structures and machinery can be used for many years. Also stimulating the economy: people purchasing or renting new residences frequently purchase new appliances and furniture.

During five years just prior to the wars in Afghanistan and Iraq (through 2000), military expenditures relative to investment were at their lowest point in the last quarter century, but were still equal to approximately one-quarter of gross private investment and one-third of business investment.[8] During the last five years, with the wars in full force, there was a significant growth in military spending. The housing boom during the same period meant that official military expenditures for 2001–05 averaged 28 percent of gross private investment—not that different from the previous period. However, when residential construction is omitted, official military outlays during the last five years were equivalent to 42 percent of gross non-residential private investment.[9]

The rate of annual increases in consumer expenditures fall somewhat with recessions and rise as the economy recovers—but still increases from year to year. However, the swings in private investment are what drive the business cycle—periods of relatively high growth alternating with periods of very slow or negative growth. In the absence of the enormous military budget, a huge increase in private investment would be needed to keep the economy from falling into a deep recession. Even with the recent sharp increases in military spending and the growth of private housing construction, the lack of rapid growth in business investment has led to a sluggish economy.

THE ROLE OF DEBT IN STIMULATING ECONOMIC GROWTH

The creation of debt in both government and private sectors also boosts the economy. Deficit spending by the government is one of the Keynesian answers to recessions, putting new dollars into circulation to create "demand." (Experience from the United States during the Great Depression as well as the recent example of Japan indicates that Keynesian debt spending does not in itself solve problems of severe economic downturns. It was not Keynesianism but the Second World War that catapulted the U.S. economy out of the Great Depression.) Likewise, when a bank lends money to a company to expand its operations or to an individual to purchase a home or a car, there is more activity in the economy than would otherwise occur.

However, there are differences between consumer and corporate borrowing. When people borrow to purchase consumer goods, the purchase itself provides an immediate stimulus. Those who made and transported and sold the goods get money that they can use in turn, and usually do so immediately. There may even be a small ripple effect in the economy.

However, when corporations borrow to build more physical plant, purchase durable machinery, or start a business in the services, the effect of the spending of borrowed money continues for years as economic activity is expanded and jobs are created.

Marx expressed the accumulation of capital through investment as M–C–M′. M(oney) capital is used to purchase raw materials, machines, and labor to produce C(ommodities), which are then sold, with the capitalist receiving back M′—the original money plus Δm, the surplus value produced by labor. In the financial circuit of capital, in contrast, money makes more money directly, represented by Marx as M–M′. Although in some respects a simplification, at one time it was fairly reasonable to think of banks as primarily loaning funds that had been deposited by the public. They collected interest and principal from those who had taken on debt and paid a share to depositors. However, today's banks have themselves become massive borrowers. Financial institutions of all types now accumulate huge quantities of debt as they attempt to make money with borrowed money. This debt undertaken by financial institutions for the purpose of speculation has little to no stimulatory effect on production. Relatively few people are employed in the process of speculation (say, per billion dollars borrowed and speculated with) compared to other more productive uses for that capital. Profits resulting from these debt-financed transactions rarely are turned into investment in factories or service sector firms that create jobs. Rather, such speculative profits are normally used to generate even more profits through various other speculation schemes, or for high living by the rich. As a result, stagnation in employment in recent years has gone hand in hand with a new opulence among the main beneficiaries of the financial expansion.

THE DEBT EXPLOSION

The rapid expansion of debt in the U.S. economy—much greater than the expansion of economic activity (as measured by increased Gross Domestic Product, or GDP)—was dramatically described by Magdoff and Sweezy in their introduction to *Stagnation and the Financial Explosion*. However, it turns out that what they observed in the early to mid-1980s was only an early portent of what was to be an unprecedented upsurge of debt in the economy (see Chart 2.1).[10] The divergence between the growth in outstanding debt in the economy and the underlying economic growth is truly astounding. In the 1970s outstanding debt was about one and a half times the size of the country's annual economic activity (GDP). By 1985, about the time that they were increasingly focused on the subject, it was twice as large as the GDP. By 2005 total U.S. debt was almost three and a half times the nation's GDP (see Chart 2.2), and not far from the $44 trillion GDP for the entire world.

Total debt in the United States is composed of debt owed by households, government (local, state, and federal), non-financial businesses, and financial institutions. While there has been near continuous-growth in debt since the late 1970s, there were bursts of debt growth relative to GDP—in the period 1981–88 (when Magdoff and Sweezy published many articles on the subject), and then again in 1997–2005. In the 1980s, the sectors with the greatest increases in debt relative to GDP were finan-

CHART 2.1: *GDP and Total Debt*

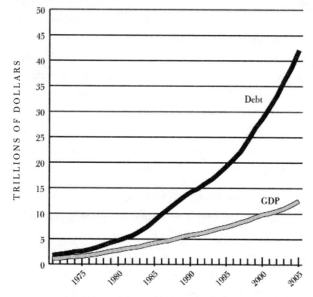

Source: Calculated from Federal Reserve, Flow of Funds Accounts of the United States, Tables L. 1 and L. 2; *Economic Report of the President, 2006,* Table B-78.

cial institutions, whose debt grew from 22 to 42 percent of the GDP in 1981–88, and government debt, which grew from 44 to 69 percent of the GDP in the same period. During the second debt burst, 1997–2005, financial business debt grew even more as a percentage of the GDP, exploding from 66 percent to over 100 percent of the GDP. During this second period household debt also shot up, from 67 to 92 percent of the GDP, in large measure because of home refinancing during the housing boom, and increased credit card debt. The debt of non-financial companies is continuing to grow rapidly. According to the *Wall Street Journal,* "Corporations are borrowing money at the fastest clip in several years amid a wave of leveraged buy-outs and acquisitions, rising capital expenditures and pressure from shareholders for larger dividends and share buybacks. . . . Nonfinancial companies saw their debt rise 6.3% in the 12 months that ended in the first quarter to $5.5 trillion. That is the fastest yearly growth for debt in five years. In 2005, debt increased at an average 12-month pace of 5.1%, while in 2004 debt growth was 2.7% . . . ".[11]

CHART 2.2: *Total Debt in the United States as a Percentage of the Economy*

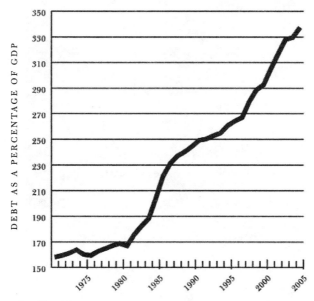

Source: See Chart 2.1.

However, it is not just non-financial corporations among today's corporations that have experienced this financial explosion. They have been outdone in recent years by their financial counterparts. Not only has the debt exploded in absolute numbers, and grown just as dramatically relative to growth in the nation's economy, its composition has changed considerably. The financial sector's debt, which accounted for about 10 percent of total U.S. debt in the early 1970s, has soared and in 2005 was close to a third of the total (Chart 2.3). The debt share of non-financial businesses and government decreased quite dramatically over the same period, while consumer debt remained at about the same proportion of total debt as it was in the economic crisis period of the mid-1970s.

As the overall debt grows larger and larger it appears to be having less of a stimulating effect on the economy. There are few places where

CHART 2.3: *Composition of United States Debt in 1975 and 2005*

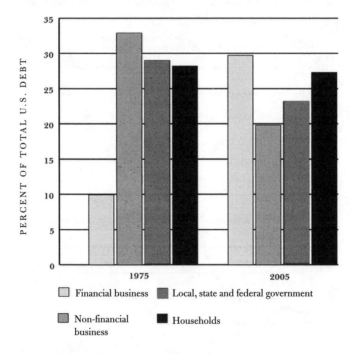

Source: See Chart 2.1.

Magdoff and Sweezy's thesis—that there is an implacable drive toward stagnation in mature capitalist economies—is clearer than in the following statistics. *Although there is no exact relationship between debt creation and economic growth, in the 1970s the increase in the GDP was about sixty cents for every dollar of increased debt. By the early 2000s this had decreased to close to twenty cents of GDP growth for every dollar of new debt.*

Debt, as we have seen, can be used for all sorts of things—some stimulates the economy greatly and has a long-lasting effect (investment in new businesses or expanding old businesses), some have a moderate and relatively short-term effect on the economy (households taking equity out of their homes or running up credit card debt to purchase consumer items), and some that has little to essentially no direct effect on the economy (financial speculation). The change in the composition of the debt, with financial sector debt now larger than any other single component and growing faster than all the rest (a shift from M–C–M´ to M–M´), may explain much of the decreased stimulation of the economy by debt expansion. Clearly, though, the tendency toward stagnation—and capital's need to look for "investments" in speculative rather than productive activities because of that stagnation—marks the current era.

It seems evident that there are both short-term and long-term limits to the rising debt/GDP ratio. Not only are periodic "credit crunches" of the kind that have shaken the financial system from time to time in recent decades inevitable, but also a major financial meltdown of a kind that the system can much less easily absorb is increasingly probable over the long run, as the financial explosion continues. As former Federal Reserve chairman Alan Greenspan told Congress in June 2005: "I think we've learned very early on in economic history that debt in modest quantities does enhance the rate of growth of an economy and does create higher standards of living, but in excess, creates very serious problems." The chief economist of MBG Information Services, Charles W. McMillion, was more straightforward—"The economy's increasing reliance on unprecedented levels of debt is clearly unsustainable and extremely troubling. . . . The only serious questions are when and how will current imbalances be addressed and what will be the consequences."[12]

There is, of course, no way to predict the level at which too much debt
might cause a deep and prolonged crisis. Stock market bubbles burst in
1987 and 2000 without slowing down this process of debt explosion,
except temporarily. How long this can continue without a much bigger,
longer lasting calamity that will reach to the core of the system is anyone's
guess—but to assume that it will continue forever is certainly wishful
thinking to an extreme. The large and steadily increasing consumer debt
relative to income is already creating difficulties for those who must pay
back their debts while sustaining their living expenses.[13] Last year U.S.
households spent a record 13.75 percent of their after-tax, or disposable,
income on servicing their debts. With little to no income growth among
wage earners, the past year (July 2005–June 2006) has seen people
spending $1.1 trillion more than they earned.[14] This negative personal
savings rate is unprecedented in the years since the Great Depression.
U.S. household debt hit a record $11.4 trillion in last year's third quarter,
which ended September 30, 2005, after shooting up at the fastest rate
since 1985, according to Federal Reserve data. Total household debt
stood at $11.8 trillion at the end of March 2006.[15]

This acceleration of household debt has been aided in large part by
the Federal Reserve in response to the stock market implosion in 2000.
When the Fed reduced interest rates to historically low levels to keep the
economy from falling into a deep recession, households increased borrowing on homes, cars, and credit cards. Household mortgage debt
increased 75 percent from 2000 to 2005 as homeowners refinanced and
obtained larger mortgages—pulling money out of their homes to use for
various purposes. As new people participated in the housing boom
homes sold at increasingly inflated prices to those with low credit ratings.
This had the effect of shifting the stock price bubble to a bubble of home
prices. This stimulated the economy, with investment in private housing
increasing to 36 percent of total private investment in 2005—a level not
seen since 1958 during the great suburban housing boom resulting from
the second wave of automobilization.

Americans have been purchasing new homes and going into more
debt by obtaining new mortgages on existing homes in which they take

on a larger mortgage based on the appreciated value of their houses. In addition, new types of mortgages have been developed for those who cannot really afford to purchase housing ("sub-prime" mortgages, at higher rates of interest, but with "come-ons" to make them look afford-able). These include mortgages in which very low interest rates are charged for a few years before the rates become adjustable and/or those in which 100 percent of the house value is financed. If interest rates increase substantially—a real possibility—the cost of past borrowing will bring major pain to many households, with increased mortgage foreclosures and bankruptcies and rising late fees and rate hikes on credit card debt. We are already witnessing the beginning of this phe-nomenon as those relying on adjustable-rate mortgages and people who borrowed 100 percent of the value of their homes are now facing the twin problems of higher mortgage payments at the same time that house values in some locales are declining.[16] Foreclosures have increased dra-matically in 2006—even among those with good credit ratings. Nonetheless, there's lots of money being made with these types of mort-gages by the mortgage brokers, the banks that originally loan the money, the loan distributors, and the hedge funds and institutional investors that purchase these loans packaged with higher-quality ones. As *Business Week* put it: "In this game almost every player wins—except for the cash-strapped homeowner."[17]

There is not enough space here to go into all of the implications of the enormous federal debt in the United States, which have been widely reported. In the last years of the Clinton administration the convergence of fiscal restraint and a speculative bubble mainly in information technol-ogy stocks led to federal budget surpluses. Since President Bush took office, annual federal deficits—and the federal debt—have grown massive-ly. This government borrowing, in large measure to "pay" for tax cuts to the wealthy (redistributing income upward) and for costly wars in Afghanistan and Iraq, is one leg of the so-called twin deficit. The other leg is the current accounts deficit.

Since 1980 there has been an almost continuous negative balance of trade between the United States and other countries. For the past two years the U.S. current account deficit has been about $700 billion, approximately 6 percent of the GDP. This means that approximately $2 billion per day must come into the United States to purchase U.S. government bonds or other assets such as stocks and real estate in order to offset the net money the U.S. population and U.S. companies send abroad for manufactured products, services, and investment. There is serious fear among financial experts that foreign central banks and wealthy individuals might direct their investments to other countries and currencies. In a recent report, the International Monetary Fund reiterated their concern about the U.S. current account imbalance: "The risk of a disorderly dollar adjustment could well increase without policies being put into place to foster the needed adjustments in saving and investment imbalances."[18]

To give an idea of what could be in store, a seemingly innocuous comment by the central bank of South Korea in February 2005—that it was planning on diversifying its foreign currency holdings away from dollar-based assets—sent the dollar into a temporary decline. As a *New York Times* editorial described it: ". . . the sell-off of dollars did not precipitate a meltdown. But it sure gave a taste of one. The dollar suffered its worst single-day decline in two months against the yen and the euro. Stock markets in New York, London, Paris, and Frankfurt dropped, and gold and oil prices, which tend to go up when the dollar goes down, spiked."[19] With South Korea holding only $69 billion in U.S. Treasuries at the time, imagine what might happen if central banks in China or Japan, holding about a trillion dollars of Treasuries, decided to shift away from the dollar! (Perhaps the only thing holding them back is that they have such huge amounts invested in dollars that their U.S.-based "savings" would be caught in any meltdown that might occur.)

THE GIANT CASINO

Along with the explosion of debt has come the exceptional growth of finance and financial speculation in the U.S. economy—stimulated significantly by increasingly higher levels of debt. As we will see below, debt helps to fuel financial speculation and at the same time financial speculation leads to more debt!

With profits from new investments more difficult to make in the "real" economy (where something is actually made or a service delivered) of mature capitalist production, another of capital's responses to stagnation has been the expansion of the financial system, along with many new gimmicks designed to appropriate surplus value from the rest of the economy.

Because they didn't know how to invest the funds, in mid-2006 U.S. corporations held the equivalent of 20 percent of their stock market value as cash and Treasuries. Moreover, surplus capital is not just an issue in the United States. Even with supposed investment opportunities in growing economies like China and India, a *Wall Street Journal* article described a huge quantity of "money sloshing around the world"—as a result of effectively interest-free money available in Japan and the United States, low interest rates in Europe, and massive amounts of "petrodollars" generated by high oil prices.[20] This is a situation, as we know from the passage cited earlier, that Marx anticipated. The financial sector now has the onus of providing new and expanded outlets for the massive hoard of capital.

Mainstream economists generally ignored stagnation and failed therefore to recognize the structural roots of the financial explosion or its dangers. In sharp contrast, Magdoff and Sweezy identified early on the critical importance of the growing role of the financial sector in the stagnating late twentieth-century economy. As they explained, with the development of giant corporations toward the end of the nineteenth century "the composition of the capitalist economy underwent a qualitative transformation. The issuance of many types and quantities of corporate securities brought in its train the development of organized stock and bond markets, brokerage houses, new forms of banking, and a community of what Veblen called captains of finance who soon rose to the top of the capitalist hierarchy of wealth and power."[21] They went on to describe the incredible pace of development in the financial sector through the twentieth century up until the period of the 1980s, when they were writing, calling this growth a "financial explosion." The last twenty years have only confirmed this assessment.

FROM M–C–M´ TO M–M´

Finance (banks, investment firms, insurance companies, and real estate consortia) develops an ever-growing number of new ways to try to make money with money—M–M´ in Marx's formulation. Thus, finance is not only the "glue" that connects the various parts of the capitalist system and the "oil" that lubricates its workings, finance has become a dominant activity in mature capitalist economies.

As discussed above, close to a third of all debt in the United States is owed by financial institutions—the largest debt sector. Of course, the point of finance taking on all that debt is to try to make money—and so it has. While in the 1960s financial profits accounted for about 15 percent of all domestic profits in the United States, by 2005 it accounted for close to 40 percent of all profits (see Chart 2.4). At the same time, manufacturing, which once accounted for 50 percent of domestic profits, now accounts for less than 15 percent of profits. Surprisingly, this shift was, if anything, even more dramatic after the 2000 stock market meltdown. (It is important to keep in mind that while manufacturing sector employment has decreased and manufacturing has become less important in producing profits than the service and financial sectors, increases in productivity have allowed the actual output of manufactured goods in the United States to continue to increase!)

The importance of finance even to non-financial corporations can be seen by examining the bottom line of many major manufacturers and retailers. As explained in *Business Week*, "At Deere & Co., the farm-equipment company, finance produces nearly one-fourth of earnings. Retailer Target Corp. (TGT) usually gets about 15% of its earnings from its credit cards. And while General Motors Corporation (GM) is having trouble selling cars, its ditech.com mortgage business is going great guns. GM's financing operations earned $2.9 billion last year, while GM lost money on cars."[22] Even the giant retailer of consumer goods Wal-Mart has gotten into the act and has begun offering a variety of financial services such as bill payment, check cashing, money orders, and wiring money to other countries.

Financial companies have developed ways to divert much of their loan-provision risk. They now "package" a group of loans together and sell them to hedge funds and other institutional investors. They earn fees for arranging the transactions and, though they collect less in interest payments, their risk is close to zero. How important is this new strategy? "Financial companies now get about 42% of their revenues from fees and only 58% from interest, compared with 20% and 80%, respectively, in 1980 . . . ".[23] No longer responsible for defaults, banks are pushing more loans, and therefore debt. Banks used to be very conservative when lending money because they wanted to insure repayment. However, the situation has changed to allow more questionable loans:

> "Banks used to want to see you be more conservative," says Daniel O'Connell, chief executive of Vestar Capital Partners, a major private-equity firm. "Now they encourage us" to borrow more. The banks are more aggressive because they rarely keep the loans they make. Instead, they sell them to others, who then repackage, or securitize, the loans and

CHART 2.4: *Five-Year Running Average of Manufacturing and Financial Sectors as a Percent of Domestic Profits*

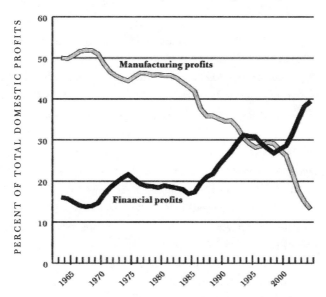

Source: Calculated from *Economic Report of the President, 2006*, Table B-91.

sell them to investors in exotic-sounding vehicles, such as CLOs, or collateralized-loan obligations. Every week brings announcements of billions of dollars in new CLOs, created by traditional money-management
and hedge funds, which then sell them to other investors. In many cases,
they may keep some slices of these complicated securities.[24]

THE MAGNITUDE OF SPECULATION

The magnitude of speculation in all manner of financial "instruments"
such as stocks, futures, derivatives, and currency is truly astonishing.
Magdoff and Sweezy were clearly astounded by this tendency when they
first sounded the alarm. Today financial analysts frequently pretend that
finance can levitate forever at higher and higher levels independently of
the underlying productive economy. Stock markets and currency trading
(betting that one nation's currency will change relative to another) have
become little more than giant casinos where the number and values of
transactions have increased far out of proportion to the underlying economy. For example, in 1975, 19 million stock shares traded daily on the
New York Stock Exchange. By 1985 the volume had reached 109 million, and by 2006, 1,600 million shares with a value of over $60 billion.[25]

Even larger is the daily trading on the world currency markets, which
has gone from $18 billion a day in 1977, to the current average of $1.8
trillion a day! *That means that every twenty-four days the dollar volume
of currency trading equals the entire world's annual GDP!* Currency
speculation is especially attractive—you can trade twenty-four hours a
day and it's easy to get in and out quickly. However, "foreign-exchange
veterans warn that the risks are huge. Traders can leverage their posi-
tions to place bets valued at as much as 200 times the money they put
up. If a bet goes wrong, they can lose by a corresponding amount."[26]
Although almost all currency trading is in major currencies such as the
dollar, the yen, the euro, and the pound sterling, one relatively recent
gambit involved borrowing Japanese yen, because the government had
been trying to stimulate its economy by having effectively zero interest
rates. These funds were then moved to countries with relatively high
interest rates like Australia, New Zealand, Turkey, and Iceland. So much
money moved into Iceland to take advantage of the 11.5 percent interest

rate on the krona, that when it began to be withdrawn after Japan indicated it was going to raise interest rates, the krona and the Icelandic stock market fell dramatically.

There are all sorts of ways to play the market game. For example, one can bet on the price of a particular stock going down (short selling) by selling borrowed stock and agreeing to repurchase the stock and return it to its owner at a particular time in the future. One can buy the right to purchase a stock in the future at a particular price (a call option), or sell a stock in the future (a put option) at a particular price.

Then there are futures—one can bet on the future value or index of almost anything. There has long been a futures market for agricultural commodities such as grains, milk, butter, coffee, sugar, orange juice, cattle, pork bellies, as well as fuels and metals. It makes a lot of sense in the productive economy for a company to stabilize or lock-in the costs of an important ingredient of their product, such as wheat for a baker. However, on a world basis, of the approximately ten billion contracts (futures, options on futures, and options on securities) traded in 2005, less than 8 percent were on agricultural commodities, metals, and energy. Nowadays about 92 percent of bets on futures are placed in the financial sector: the prices of different currencies, municipal and Treasury bonds, stocks, interest rates, and various financial or stock indices (such as the Japanese NIKKEI 225, the U.S. Standard & Poors 500, and Dow Jones Industrial Average, etc.).

One of the more bizarre futures markets was created in 2003 by the U.S. government's Department of Defense along with a private company—betting on the likelihood of assassinations and terrorist attacks. As then Senate minority leader Tom Daschle, D-South Dakota, said on the Senate floor: "I couldn't believe that we would actually commit $8 million to create a Web site that would encourage investors to bet on futures involving terrorist attacks and public assassinations . . . I can't believe that anybody would seriously propose that we trade in death . . . How long would it be before you saw traders investing in a way that would bring about the desired result?" The uproar resulted in the canceling of the government's participation in the program.

Derivatives and hedge funds have also played a critical role in the explosion of financial speculation.

The daily turnover of foreign exchange and interest rate derivate contracts (including traditional instruments such as outright forwards and foreign exchange swaps) between April 2001 and April 2004 increased by an estimated 74 percent, to $2.4 trillion. The notional amounts of over-the-counter derivatives (the sum of the nominal absolute value of all deals concluded and still open) at the end of June 2006 was $283 trillion—more than six times all the goods and services produced in the world during a year's time. To give some idea of the continuing pace of derivative activity, during the first half of 2006 "the global market in credit derivatives grew 52 percent, to $26 trillion."[27] This market has grown at a pace of over 100 percent a year during the last four years.

U.S.-based hedge funds, currently with assets of approximately $1.2 trillion, quickly move large amounts of capital into and out of investments—it's estimated that they do about half of the daily trading of stocks in the United States. And while they claim high returns, there are many dangers lurking behind the big chances these funds are taking. For example, the hedge fund Amaranth Advisors lost $6 billion, more than half of its assets under management, during one week in September. They lost so much money so rapidly by placing large bets on the price of natural gas, which is a lot more volatile than the price of oil. They bet that the price difference between gas for delivery in March 2007 and gas for delivery a month later (April 2007) would continue to widen. Instead, as gas prices generally decreased in September, the spread narrowed significantly. Clearly, this type of speculation creates potential instability in the financial system. As an article in the *New York Times* put it: "Enormous losses at one of the nation's largest hedge funds resurrected worries yesterday that major bets by these secretive, unregulated investment partnerships could create widespread financial disruptions."[28]

MERGERS AND ACQUISITIONS (M&A)

We are in the midst of a frenzy of acquisitions of companies by other companies and buyouts in which private investment firms acquire corporations. Most of these involve a significant amount of leverage (borrowing), thus adding to the overall debt in the system. An article on Forbes.com last year explained, "The feverish pace of activity [of leveraged buyouts] is a tribute to the reality that investors are scrounging for any sort of deal that will get them a better return on their money than long-term Treasuries can give them."[29] This year we are on a pace to exceed the $3 trillion total value of mergers and acquisitions at the height of the last frenzy in 2000.[30] The activity has been especially large for a number of reasons, primary among which is the amount of capital sloshing around in the system. As the *Wall Street Journal* put it: "The piles of cash and stockpile of repurchased shares at . . . companies have hit record levels and continue to grow along with corporate earnings, creating challenges for the executives who must decide how to allocate all that capital."[31]

Buyouts of corporations by private investment groups supposedly add value as the new managers improve a troubled company and then sell new stock to public investors. However, in the current environment it is not uncommon for private capital to, in the words of a *Business Week* headline, "Buy it, Strip it, Then Flip it."[32] Income can be generated very quickly in these deals. For example, the private investment firms that purchased Burger King Corporation in 2002 actually used their own money for only one-third of the $1.4 billion purchase price. Where did the rest of the money come from? It came as debt taken on by the Burger King Corporation. This extra debt allowed Burger King to pay the new owners $448 million in "dividends and fees" including "$55 million in interest on their loan, which the company repaid early with new borrowings."[33] So the private equity firms essentially got their money back in the process of acquiring a 76 percent stake in Burger King, now estimated to be worth $1.8 billion—more than three times their initial investment! Purchasers of the company's stock, meanwhile, are buying a large debt load that had not been there previously.

In a more recent deal, the for-profit hospital chain HCA is being purchased by "three private-equity firms—Bain, Kohlberg Kravis and Merrill Lynch's buyout unit—and the Frist family [that together] are investing only $5.5 billion in cash. The rest of the $31.6 billion price tag is being financed by debt, which the firms will hope to pay down, like a mortgage payment, using HCA's income."[34] (One of the central members of that Frist family is the majority leader of the U.S. Senate and a widely reported possible candidate for president in 2008.)

According to Standard & Poor's, over the last three years, "companies have borrowed $69 billion primarily to pay dividends to private-equity owners. . . . That compares with $10 billion in the previous six years."[35] And buyouts through July of 2006 were close to $200 billion, about double the amount for the full year of 2004. In essence, capital is using the vast surplus at its disposal not to invest in new productive capacity, but in corporate buyouts aimed at increasing their financial claims to wealth.

These leveraged buyouts are creating more debt at the same time they create huge profits for speculators. Whether the companies they purchased through leveraged buyouts are made more profitable before being sold back to the public through the issuance of new stock is debatable. What is not debatable is that the taken-private companies are laden with debt.

According to the *Wall Street Journal*,

> Twenty percent [of corporations selling stock through IPOs—initial public offerings] carried net tangible book-value deficits even after raising money through their IPOs, meaning that, if those companies were liquidated the day they came public, stockholders would receive nothing. The majority of debt-heavy companies went public as a result of the private-equity investment process. Private-equity firms, such as Apollo Management LP and Cypress Group, are behind 40% of the IPOs . . . this year. They often purchase companies by investing some cash and leveraging the rest of the asking price, with the debt landing on the balance sheets of their new acquisitions. [36]

FINANCIAL CAPITAL'S NEW BOTTOM LINE

Currency and futures speculation, trading in complex derivatives, the emergence and growth of hedge funds, and the stunning increase in debt are all responses to the same phenomenon. As the economy of production of goods and services stagnates, failing to generate the rate of return from M–C–M′ that capital desires, a new type of "investment" has emerged. It seeks to leverage debt and embrace bubble-like expansions aimed at high, speculative profits through financial instruments. The depth of stagnation, and its tenacious hold on the mature capitalist economy, is amply testified to by the flight of investment into what we have called "the giant casino." The reduction of real wages (adjusted for inflation) and the redistribution of wealth upward (through reduced taxes and reductions in social services)—the results of class war waged unilaterally from above—have not been enough to guarantee an ever-increasing spiral of return on capital invested in the productive economy. Thus, continual recourse to new forms of gambling, not production of goods or services, is what capital is generating in the pursuit of profit.

The huge expansion of debt and speculation provide ways to extract more surplus from the general population and are, thus, part of capital's exploitation of workers and the lower middle class. A number of capital's techniques have been discussed above: (a) extending more and more loans to the general public and corporations; (b) lending to low-income people under very unfavorable and hard to understand terms; (c) adding debt to corporations through leveraged buyouts (making the companies more financially fragile and demanding cutbacks in jobs, wages, and benefits to compensate); (d) unbalancing trade with the rest of the world, requiring enormous sums of money to be invested in the U.S. from abroad; and (e) placing huge bets on almost anything imaginable. A lot of people are making money off of these activities—except for those at the bottom who are left to foot the bill when problems arise. An idea of how much the general public has to pay for the financial shenanigans that capital plays—as the cost of failure is passed down from capital to the public—is indicated by the U.S. government bailout of the savings and loan industry in the 1990s which cost somewhere around $175 billion, adding to current and future personal tax obligations!

There is growing concern about the potential consequences of the growth in debt and speculation and changes in the financial system.[37]

The president of the New York Federal Reserve Bank, Timothy Geithner, feels that the changes in the financial system since 1998 (and the selling of debt obligations to numerous buyers) have lessened the chances that relatively small shocks will upset the entire system. Yet, "the same factors," he wrote, "that may have reduced the probability of future systemic events . . . may amplify the damage caused by and complicate the management of very severe financial shocks. The changes that have reduced the vulnerability of the system to smaller shocks may have increased the severity of the large ones."[38]

Numerous sources of fragility are introduced into the U.S. economy by the various techniques capital uses to try to overcome the obstacles to profitable opportunities caused by stagnation. These have created trends that cannot continue without generating bigger contradictions in the future: the huge annual imbalances of trade between the United States and the rest of the world; ever expanding debt in all sectors of the economy *relative to the underlying economy*; the shift of the financial sector into ever larger-scale speculation. There are limits (though not easily discerned) to the size of the financial superstructure relative to the productive base. Although devised as ad hoc ways to cope with stagnation, such speculative "solutions" cannot continue to expand the system, balloon-like forever. The only questions are how will it all end and where will capital turn when these mechanisms have run their course? One possibility is a severe and long lasting recession with generalized deflation. Another is that the government continues successfully to intervene to bail out the financial system when it gets into trouble such as with the banking system failures in the 1980s and the near collapse of Long Term Capital Management in the late 1990s. However, with the magnitude of the intertwined debt and speculation so enormous, it is clear that these types of interventions can bail out the system at most only temporarily, while extending the overall crisis and the long-term threat to the economy.

3. Monopoly-Finance Capital

December 2006

The year now ending marks the fortieth anniversary of Paul Baran and Paul Sweezy's classic work, *Monopoly Capital: An Essay on the American Economic and Social Order*. Compared to mainstream economic works of the early to mid-1960s (the most popular and influential of which were John Kenneth Galbraith's *New Industrial State* and Milton Friedman's *Capitalism and Freedom*), *Monopoly Capital* stood out not simply in its radicalism but also in its historical specificity. What Baran and Sweezy sought to explain was not capitalism as such, the fundamental account of which was to be found in Marx's *Capital*, but rather a particular *stage* of capitalist development. Their stated goal was nothing less than to provide a brief "essay-sketch" of the monopoly stage of capitalism by examining the interaction of its basic economic tendencies, narrowly conceived, with the historical, political, and social forces that helped to shape and support them.

Hence, the most important question to address on the fortieth anniversary of Baran and Sweezy's book is: Has capitalism changed, evolving still further within or even beyond the monopoly stage as they described it? There is of course no easy answer to this question. As in the case of all major historical developments what is most evident in retrospect is the contradictory nature of the changes that have taken place since the mid-1960s. On the one hand, it is clear that the system has not yet found a way to move forward with respect to its driving force: the process of capital accumulation. The stagnation impasse described in *Monopoly Capital* has worsened: the underlying disease has spread and deepened while new corrosive symptoms have come into being. On the other hand, the system has found new ways of reproducing itself, and capital has paradoxically even prospered within this impasse, through the explosive growth of finance, or what Sweezy was to refer to as "The Triumph of Financial Capital."[1] We will provisionally call this new hybrid phase of the system "monopoly-finance capital."[2]

In bare outline the argument of *Monopoly Capital* can be summarized as follows. At the brink of the twentieth century, capitalism underwent a major transformation, marked by the rise of the giant corporation. The early decades that followed were dominated by world wars and a depression associated with this great transformation. Following the Second World War the new stage of capitalism was fully consolidated, particularly within the United States, the most advanced capitalist economy. The result was a situation in which a handful of giant corporations controlled most industries. This constituted an enormous departure from the freely competitive system of the nineteenth century, in which the economy had been mostly made up of small, family-based firms that had little control over price, output, and investment levels—all of which were determined by larger market forces.

In the new monopoly capitalist order firms behaved not as the freely competitive enterprises of textbook economics but as what Joseph Schumpeter in *Capitalism, Socialism and Democracy* called "corespective" firms, or rational, profit-maximizing oligopolies, each of which took their main rivals into consideration in their pricing decisions, and in their attempts to increase their profit margins and market shares.[3] Such monopolistic firms abandoned mutually destructive price-competition, which was dubbed "price warfare." Instead they competed mainly in the areas of cost-cutting and the sales effort. The result was what Baran and Sweezy called a "tendency of the surplus to rise" in the economy as a whole, and particularly in that part represented by the large corporations.

This meant that the main problem of the economy was to find ways to absorb the enormous actual and potential economic surplus. In line with earlier pioneering work by Michal Kalecki and Joseph Steindl, Baran and Sweezy argued that the monopoly capitalist economy was characterized by a tendency to stagnation as profitable investment outlets for the surplus were found lacking and as other ways of absorbing surplus (such as the sales effort and government spending) were ultimately unable to pick up the slack. The resulting chronic overcapacity in production kept capital accumulation on a short leash by reducing expected profits on new investment and hence the willingness to invest.

Short of the appearance of a new epoch-making innovation that would reignite the accumulation process with the scale-effects of the steam engine, the railroad, and the automobile, the system might remain mired in stagnation indefinitely. As Kalecki put it in his *Theory of Economic Dynamics*, "Our analysis shows . . . that long-run development is not inherent in the capitalist economy. Thus specific 'development factors' are required to sustain a long-run upward movement."[4]

The pivotal issue for monopoly capital was to find additional outlets for surplus, beyond capitalist consumption and investment, that would serve to keep the system from sinking into an economic malaise. Indeed, at the time Baran and Sweezy were writing capitalism was enjoying a "golden age," a period of prosperity reminiscent of the best times of its youth. Much of their work was therefore directed at identifying those forces countering the system's stagnation tendency. Chapters 5–7 of their book examined how capitalist consumption and investment were supplemented as surplus absorbers by civilian government spending, military/imperialist expenditures, and the sales effort. However, growth of civilian government spending was strictly limited by the fact that it tended to intrude on areas of private accumulation. Military spending needed to be justified in terms of some external threat, and hence could only go so far. The sales effort was only rational at the level of the firm insofar as it translated into additional sales and increased market share. In general, Baran and Sweezy argued, there was a lack of symmetry between stagnation and those factors combating it. While the stagnation tendency was deeply rooted, powerful and persistent, the countervailing tendencies were more superficial, weaker and self-limiting.[5]

Looking back at this argument a quarter-century later in his article "*Monopoly Capital* After 25 Years," Sweezy remarked: "On the whole I think it holds up pretty well when judged in the light of all the developments and changes that have taken place in this eventful quarter-century."[6] The prosperity of the early post–Second World War decades had begun to unwind almost as soon as their book was published and the 1970s saw a return to conditions of stagnation, reminiscent of the 1930s but not so gloomy, that have remained with the U.S. and world economy ever since. *Monopoly Capital*'s bold assertion in the middle of the post–Second World War boom that "the *normal* state of the monopoly capitalist economy is stagnation," turning the usual assumption of rapid growth on its head, was therefore confirmed to a considerable extent by the subsequent historical record.[7]

Nevertheless, Sweezy on the twenty-fifth anniversary of *Monopoly Capital* saw its analysis as deeply flawed in one respect: the failure to envision the financial take off that began in the 1970s and accelerated in the 1980s. As he put it, "There is one glaring discrepancy [between the theory and actual historical development] which is not even hinted at, let alone explained, in *Monopoly Capital*. This is the burgeoning in precisely these last twenty-five years of a vastly expanded and increasingly complex financial sector in both the United States and the global capitalist economies. And this development in turn has reacted back in important ways on the structure and functioning of the corporation-dominated 'real' economy." He went on to describe three features of this financialization of the economy that modified or undermined important aspects of the *Monopoly Capital* argument.

First, the chapter on the giant corporation had assumed that the firm structure of corporate capitalism was more or less stable. The leveraged buy-out mania of the 1980s fed by junk bonds, however, changed all of that, demonstrating that even some of the largest corporations were vulnerable to outside takeovers by financial entrepreneurs. Such financial interests, led by junk bond kings, drew on huge cash reserves to court and buy out stockholders and to dump increased debt on the targeted firm once the takeover was completed, looting the acquired company. Although only relatively few giant corporations were subject to such hostile takeovers, the overall effect wrought on the corporate universe was enormous, forcing firms to load themselves down with debt in order to be less attractive to financial wolves looking for assets to leverage. Corporations as a whole took on "the coloration of speculative finance," while the previous stability of the corporate world was shaken. This, Sweezy noted, "calls into question the corporate paradigm that Baran and I treated as a built-in feature of monopoly capitalism." To some extent, control over the economy had shifted from the corporate boardrooms to the financial markets. Corporations were increasingly seen as bundles of assets, the more liquid the better.[8]

A second way in which *Monopoly Capital* came up short, Sweezy observed, was in its failure to anticipate the explosion of finance in the 1970s and '80s, which was to have far-reaching effects on the laws of motion of monopoly capital. This, he stated, had "several dimensions: the number and variety of markets [and financial instruments] involved . . . ; the dramatic expansion of activity in these markets; the absolute and relative growth in employment in financial occupations; and the increase in the share of finance in GNP. Along all these dimensions the relative size of the financial sector has grown enormously in the last two decades."

This ballooning of finance produced new outlets for surplus in the finance, insurances, and real estate (FIRE) sector of GDP in the form of new investment in buildings, office equipment, etc. Nevertheless, the great bulk of the money capital devoted to finance was used for speculation in securities, real estate, and commodities markets rather than for investment in capital goods, and thus did not feed into the growth of GDP, which continued to stagnate.

Third, the argument advanced in *Monopoly Capital*, Sweezy observed, did not foresee a shift that was to occur in the overall direction of investment. Relying on his analysis with his *MR* coeditor Harry Magdoff of "The Strange Recovery of 1983–84," he noted how business cycle recoveries traditionally took the form of strong investment in plant and equipment in manufacturing, transportation, and public utilities.[9] But these areas of investment were now seeing little rise even in the recovery stage of the business cycle in comparison to those areas such as office equipment associated with FIRE.

"Why," Sweezy asked, "did *Monopoly Capital* fail to anticipate the changes in the structure and functioning of the system that have taken place in the last twenty-five years? Basically, I think the answer is that its conceptualization of the capital accumulation process is one-sided and incomplete":

> In the established tradition of both mainstream and Marxian economics, we treated capital accumulation as being essentially a matter of adding to the stock of existing capital goods. But in reality this is only one aspect of the process. Accumulation is also a matter of adding to the stock of financial assets. The two aspects are of course interrelated, but the nature of this interrelation is problematic to say the least. The traditional way of handling the problem has been in effect to assume it away: for example, buying stocks and bonds (two of the simpler forms of financial assets) is assumed to be merely an indirect way of buying real capital goods. This is hardly ever true, and it can be totally misleading.
>
> This is not the place to try to point the way to a more satisfactory conceptualization of the capital accumulation process. It is at best an extremely complicated and difficult problem, and I am frank to say that I have no clues to its solution. But I can say with some confidence that achieving a better understanding of the monopoly capitalist society of today will be possible only on the basis of a more adequate theory of capital accumulation, with special emphasis on the interaction of its real and financial aspects, than we now possess.

Reviewing Sweezy's reassessment of *Monopoly Capital* a decade and a half further on, we believe he was too harsh a critic of his and Baran's book for what he called its "glaring discrepancy" with respect to its understanding of accumulation and finance. Far from failing to even "hint" at the role of finance, *Monopoly Capital* had included at the very end of the chapter on "The Sales Effort" a separate section on the role of the finance sector as an outlet for surplus absorption, arguing that this was "on an equal footing with the sales effort." There Baran and Sweezy stressed the "sheer magnitude" of surplus diverted into FIRE in the national accounts. This represented, they argued, nothing less than a "gigantic system of speculating, swindling, and cheating," mounting ever higher along with the rising surplus and contributing to the growing irrationality of the system.[10]

If there was one U.S. economist who was closest to Baran and Sweezy while *Monopoly Capital* was being written it was Harry Magdoff, who was party to the discussions that led to Baran and Sweezy's book, and who was to join Sweezy as coeditor of *Monthly Review* in 1969. In the 1965 issue of the *Socialist Register,* appearing at about the same time that *Monopoly Capital* was completed, Magdoff stressed the problem of the rise in credit/debt in the U.S. economy. In addition, in the final sentence of his 1967 review of *Monopoly Capital,* Magdoff wrote: "Other areas that seem to be especially pertinent to the development and testing of the Baran-Sweezy thesis are: the role of credit and speculation in the expansion and contraction of the surplus; and the interrelation between the U.S. as world banker, the dollar as an international currency, balance of payments difficulties, and the international nature of the U.S. economy."[11] It is therefore not surprising that very soon after the publication of *Monopoly Capital,* Magdoff and Sweezy were to take up all of these issues, focusing in particular on the critical problem of credit and speculation in the absorption of the surplus.

The financialization of monopoly capital, it is now apparent, represented a whole new historical period—one that no one had any inkling of in the 1960s, and that, according to existing economic doctrine, both mainstream and Marxian, remains largely inexplicable today. When the first real signs of a massive secular increase in debt appeared in the 1970s and '80s it was Magdoff and Sweezy writing for *Monthly Review* who were among the first to perceive the magnitude of the changes taking place, and who were almost alone in emphasizing the significance of the dual reality of *stagnation and the financial explosion.*[12]

Indeed, from the standpoint of today one is struck by how early Magdoff and Sweezy recognized the importance of the change taking place in the workings of capitalism. As we noted in the previous chapter and bears repeating, what they "observed in the early to mid-1980s was only an early portent of what was to be an unprecedented upsurge of debt in the economy. . . . In the 1970s [when they first pointed to the phenomenon] outstanding debt was about one and a half times the size of the country's annual economic activity (GDP). By 1985, about the time they were increasingly focused on the subject, it was twice as large as GDP. By 2005 total U.S. debt was almost three and a half times the nation's GDP and not far from the $44 trillion GDP for the entire world."[13]

The principal backdrop against which we normally view the growth of finance is production, the so-called real economy. In cutting through the usual obscurities of economic thought and focusing on the real-world tendencies of rising surplus and stagnation, *Monopoly Capital* had provided the theoretical basis with regard to production from which Sweezy and Magdoff were able to ascertain the enormity of the qualitative transformation represented by the explosion of finance almost from the moment of its inception.

Yet, if the basic argument of *Monopoly Capital*, we argue, remains crucial, there is still no avoiding Sweezy's own contention that his and Baran's book contained a flaw common to both Marxian and mainstream economic theory in its reliance on a one-sided view of the capital accumulation process. According to the argument that he advanced in the 1990s, the accumulation of capital cannot be seen as simply adding to stocks of existing capital goods. It must also be perceived as a buildup of financial claims to wealth. Moreover, the latter cannot be written off as merely a fictional mirror of the former as has been customary in economic theory, which has long distinguished between what it calls the "real" and the financial aspects of the economy—a by-product of its tendency to treat money as mainly "neutral" in its effects on the economy apart from the price level.[14] Both production and finance under capitalism are at one and the same time both real and monetary in nature.

The rise of monopoly capitalism in the late nineteenth through the twentieth century went hand in hand with the rise of the market for industrial securities, i.e., the introduction of the stock market. Traditionally, the accumulation of stocks and bonds and other financial instruments has been seen as a form of the collective pooling of savings (or surplus) for investment in production. This, however, is seldom actually the case since very little of what passes through the stock exchange and other financial markets is channeled into investment in the productive economy. The development of a massive and sophisticated system of finance associated with corporate finance and banking, centered on the stock market (which Marx already in his time saw as the basis of a vast expansion of the credit market) was a product of the desire of investors to limit their risk associated with investment within production by the holding of "paper" claims to wealth. Such paper claims were liquid and easily transferable, and thus separate from the "real" assets that resided with the corporation. "So long as it is open to the individual to employ his wealth in hoarding or lending *money*," Keynes wrote in *The General Theory*, "the alternative of purchasing actual capital assets cannot be rendered sufficiently attractive . . . except by organising markets wherein these assets can be easily realised for money."[15]

But the contradiction that this creates for accumulation is far-reaching. As Magdoff and Sweezy explained in "Production and Finance," "corporate securities acquired the attribute of liquidity—instant convertibility into cash—which the physical assets of corporations by their very nature could never have. And once this stage had been reached, the way was open for a proliferation of financial instruments and markets which, so far at any rate, has proved to be literally unlimited."[16] Focusing on this contradiction of the capitalist economy, Keynes in 1931 had noted that to a considerable extent "the actual owners of wealth [say of corporations] have claims, not on real assets, but on money. . . . The interposition of this veil of money between the real asset and the wealth owner is a specifically marked characteristic of the modern world."[17] Such a dual system of accumulation was bound to generate a rise in speculation, and an ever more layered/leveraged financial system. Under such circumstances, Keynes observed in an oft-quoted expression, the danger is that "enterprise becomes the bubble on a whirlpool of speculation."[18]

In the late 1950s and early 1960s, when *Monopoly Capital* was being written, industrial capital was still firmly in control, financing its investment through its own internal funds, and it was common to see the basis of the system at the level of the giant firm as fairly stable. But the changes that emerged with the resurfacing of stagnation altered all of that. The golden age of the 1960s was succeeded by a leaden age that dragged on seemingly endlessly with no hope of full recovery. "A new stimulus was badly needed" under these conditions, Sweezy observed in "The Triumph of Financial Capital," "and it emerged in a form which, while certainly unanticipated, was nevertheless a logical outcome of well established tendencies within the global capitalist system." Unable to find profitable outlets for their investment-seeking surplus within the productive economy, corporations/capitalists sought to augment their money capital by means of financial speculation, while the financial system in its turn responded to this increased demand for its "products" with a bewildering array of new financial instruments—including stock futures, options, derivatives, hedge funds, etc. The result was the rise by the 1980s of a financial superstructure that increasingly took on a life of its own.

Naturally, this autonomy of finance from production is of a relative rather than an absolute kind. Financial euphorias during which speculative finance seems to be breaking away from its moorings in production, inevitably lead to widespread notions of a "New Economy," as in the late 1990s, rooted in the mistaken assumption that the laws of gravity have been suspended.[19] Such financial bubbles inevitably burst in the end, as in the stock market crashes of 1987 and 2000. What Hyman Minsky, based on the work of Keynes, called "the financial instability hypothesis," according to which advanced capitalist economies inevitably shift toward progressively more fragile financial structures not supported by the underlying accumulation process, thereby generating financial crises, remains an irrefutable truth.[20] Reflecting this, a recently released collection of interviews of Wall Street financial investors and analysts is ironically entitled *What Goes Up*.[21]

Nevertheless, what is most startling, looking back on the last two decades since the 1987 stock market crash, is that the major financial meltdowns over the period did little to halt the long-run growth of debt as a percent of GDP in the U.S. economy, which continued to skyrocket with only brief pauses after the financial blowouts. While the stock market lost nearly 50 percent of its value (in terms of the Standard and Poor 500) between March 2000 and October 2002, it had regained around half that loss two years later.[22] Debt, meanwhile, continued its inexorable rise. The economic shock from the bursting of the stock market bubble was eased by the expansion of the debt bubble in housing prices, based on speculation in the housing market—a bubble that has now been pricked by rising interest rates, slowing down economic growth.[23] Doubtless other bubbles will follow only to burst in the end.

None of this is to deny of course that a much bigger financial shock and debt-deflation might have a more lasting effect—producing a severe form of stagnation that alters the rules of the game. In Japan a major financial crash at the beginning of the 1990s contributed to what was called "The Great Stagnation," in which that country has been mired for more than a decade.[24]

A lot depends not on conditions in the United States alone but on the global economy and the global financial system. World production as a whole is characterized by slow growth, surplus capacity, and an ever greater polarization, with the poorest of the poor (especially in Africa) sinking into a horror of immiseration and plummeting life expectancy. Meanwhile, the massive U.S. current account deficit has made it the world's largest debtor economy. This means that there is a surfeit of dollars globally. China alone holds no less than a trillion U.S. dollars in its foreign reserves. Under these circumstances of increasing global financial fragility centered on the dollar, it is not difficult to envision a meltdown of truly earth-shaking proportions. The Asian financial crisis of 1997–98 gave some indication of how fast financial contagion can spread.

But if a global debt meltdown and debt-deflation is certainly one possibility at present, another is that the dual contradiction of stagnation and financial explosion will be prolonged indefinitely, barring some major external shock to the system. The Federal Reserve and the central banks of other leading capitalist states are prepared to pump liquidity quickly into the system at any sign of a major financial disruption, acting as lenders of last resort. The possibility that they might be able to prop up this whole shaky structure for some time to come cannot therefore be entirely discounted. The question then arises: What are the likely consequences of a long-run continuation of the financial explosion of the last three decades? Historical experience suggests that while the financial expansion has helped to absorb surplus it has not been able to lift the productive economy out of stagnation to any appreciable degree—so the two realities of stagnation and financial explosion coexist. As *Business Week* once editorialized, "Slow growth and today's rampant speculative binge are locked in some kind of symbiotic embrace."[25] Making money increasingly displaces making goods (and services) and the latter is consequently dwindling in proportion.

Indeed, bigger and bigger injections of debt now seem to be necessary to stimulate a given growth of GDP. As we noted in the previous chapter, "Although there is no exact relationship between debt creation and economic growth, in the 1970s the increase in the GDP was about sixty cents for every dollar of increased debt. By the early 2000s this had decreased to close to twenty cents of GDP growth for every dollar of new debt."

A system geared to speculation under conditions of increasing financial fragility needs constant new infusions of cash, much of which is obtained from the working population through drastic increases in exploitation. For most U.S. workers the economic contradictions of monopoly-finance capital have created a situation something like the closing of a vise grip. Real wages for most workers have been stagnant for a generation or more; household debt is rising as a proportion of disposable income; unemployment/underemployment has climbed; labor force participation is falling (reflecting weak job creation and the discouragement this engenders); health care benefits, pensions, and governmental services to the population (including education) are all in decline; and the share of taxes paid by workers is expanding. It would seem from all of this that under monopoly-finance capital "an accumulation of misery" is "a necessary condition, corresponding to the accumulation of wealth."[26]

One issue that urgently needs to be addressed is the specific relation of the new phase of monopoly-finance capital to imperialism. The present decade has seen the emergence of a new naked imperialism, marked by U.S. wars in Iraq and Afghanistan, an expansion of U.S. military bases globally, and a big jump in U.S. military spending. Washington's aggression is aimed primarily at regaining some of the lost U.S. hegemony over the world economy. But behind this imperialist expansion there are also deep-seated concerns at the top of the U.S. global empire over economic stagnation, control of the world's oil supply and other strategic resources, and the bases of financial dominance and stability (including the hegemony of the dollar).

Moreover, this new naked imperialism is an extension of tendencies already visible in neoliberal globalization that arose in response to the spread of stagnation in the 1970s and '80s, and that took a particularly virulent form with the onset of the third world debt crisis in the early 1980s. There is no doubt that monopoly-finance capital requires enhanced intrusion into the economic and social life of the poor countries for the purpose of extracting ever greater surplus from the periphery. Third world countries have long experienced an enormous net outflow of surplus in the form of net payments to foreign investors and lenders located in the center of the world system. These and other payments for services (for example freight charges owed to capital in the rich countries) have a negative effect on the current account balances of underdeveloped countries and tend to pull them into the red irrespective of the trade balance, which is also normally stacked against them.[27] Neoliberal economic restructuring, characteristic of the age of global monopoly-finance capital, only worsens this overall situation, removing whatever limited controls peripheral economies had on international capital in their countries and whatever limited supports were established for their own populations. Such neoliberal restructuring is spearheaded by the economic troika of the IMF/World Bank/WTO, and by the governments and corporations of the center countries. But it is ultimately backed by the military forces in the advanced capitalist states, particularly the U.S. gendarme, which exceeds in the production of means of destruction all of the other imperial powers put together. If history is any guide, the current revolt emerging against neoliberalism throughout the periphery will be met with increased interventions from the imperial center of the system, led by the United States.

Four decades after the publication of *Monopoly Capital* the contradictions of capitalism depicted there have metamorphosed into altogether more destructive forms. There is no existing economic theory that adequately explains the phase of monopoly-finance capital. But the specific answer to "the irrational system" that Baran and Sweezy provided in the closing sentences of their book (which they dedicated to their friend Che) is now more pertinent than ever: "What we in the United States need is historical perspective, courage to face the facts, and faith in mankind and its future. Having these, we can recognize our moral obligation to devote ourselves to fighting against an evil and destructive system which maims, oppresses, and dishonors those who live under it, and which threatens devastation and death to millions . . . around the globe."

4. The Financialization of Capitalism
April 2007

Changes in capitalism over the last three decades have been commonly characterized using a trio of terms: neoliberalism, globalization, and financialization. Although a lot has been written on the first two of these, much less attention has been given to the third.[1] Yet, financialization is now increasingly seen as the dominant force in this triad. The financialization of capitalism—the shift in gravity of economic activity from production (and even from much of the growing service sector) to finance—is thus one of the key issues of our time. More than any other phenomenon it raises the question: has capitalism entered a new stage?

We will argue that although the system has changed as a result of financialization, this falls short of a whole new stage of capitalism, since the basic problem of accumulation within production remains the same. Instead, financialization has resulted in a new hybrid phase of the monopoly stage of capitalism that might be termed "monopoly-finance capital."[2] Rather than advancing in a fundamental way, capital is trapped in a seemingly endless cycle of stagnation and financial explosion. These new economic relations of monopoly-finance capital have their epicenter in the United States, still the dominant capitalist economy, but have increasingly penetrated the global system.

The origins of the term "financialization" are obscure, although it began to appear with increasing frequency in the early 1990s.[3] The fundamental issue of a gravitational shift toward finance in capitalism as a whole, however, has been around since the late 1960s. The earliest figures on the left (or perhaps anywhere) to explore this question systematically were Harry Magdoff and Paul Sweezy, writing for *Monthly Review*.[4]

As Robert Pollin, a major analyst of financialization who teaches economics at the University of Massachusetts at Amherst, has noted: "beginning in the late 1960s and continuing through the 1970s and 1980s" Magdoff and Sweezy documented "the emerging form of capitalism that has now become ascendant—the increasing role of finance in the operations of capitalism. This has been termed 'financialization,' and I think it's fair to say that Paul and Harry were the first people on the left to notice this and call attention [to it]. They did so with their typical cogency, command of the basics, and capacity to see the broader implications for a Marxist understanding of reality." As Pollin remarked on a later occasion: "Harry [Magdoff] and Paul Sweezy were true pioneers in recognizing this trend. . . . [A] major aspect of their work was the fact that these essays [in *Monthly Review* over three decades] tracked in simple but compelling empirical detail the emergence of financialization as a phenomenon. . . . It is not clear when people on the left would have noticed and made sense of these trends without Harry, along with Paul, having done so first."[5]

FROM STAGNATION TO FINANCIALIZATION

In analyzing the financialization of capitalism, Magdoff and Sweezy were not mere chroniclers of a statistical trend. They viewed this through the lens of a historical analysis of capitalist development. Perhaps the most succinct expression of this was given by Sweezy in 1997, in an article entitled "More (or Less) on Globalization." There he referred to what he called "the three most important underlying trends in the recent history of capitalism, the period beginning with the recession of 1974–75: (1) the slowing down of the overall rate of growth, (2) the worldwide proliferation of monopolistic (or oligopolistic) multinational corporations, and (3) what may be called the financialization of the capital accumulation process."

For Sweezy these three trends were "intricately interrelated." Monopolization tends to swell profits for the major corporations while also reducing "the demand for additional investment in increasingly controlled markets." The logic is one of "more and more profits, fewer and fewer profitable investment opportunities, a recipe for slowing down capital accumulation and therefore economic growth which is powered by capital accumulation."

The resulting "double process of faltering real investment and burgeoning financialization" as capital sought to find a way to utilize its economic surplus, first appeared with the waning of the "'golden age' of the post Second World War decades and has persisted," Sweezy observed, "with increasing intensity to the present."[6]

This argument was rooted in the theoretical framework provided by Paul Baran and Paul Sweezy's *Monopoly Capital* (1966), which was inspired by the work of economists Michal Kalecki and Josef Steindl— and going further back by Karl Marx and Rosa Luxemburg.[7] The monopoly capitalist economy, Baran and Sweezy suggested, is a vastly productive system that generates huge surpluses for the tiny minority of monopolists/oligopolists who are the primary owners and chief beneficiaries of the system. As capitalists they naturally seek to invest this surplus in a drive to ever greater accumulation. But the same conditions that give rise to these surpluses also introduce barriers that limit their profitable investment. Corporations can just barely sell the current level of goods to consumers at prices calibrated to yield the going rate of oligopolistic profit. The weakness in the growth of consumption results in cutbacks in the utilization of productive capacity as corporations attempt to avoid overproduction and price reductions that threaten their profit margins. The consequent buildup of excess productive capacity is a warning sign for business, indicating that there is little room for investment in new capacity.

For the owners of capital the dilemma is what to do with the immense surpluses at their disposal in the face of a dearth of investment opportunities. Their main solution from the 1970s on was to expand their demand for financial products as a means of maintaining and expanding their money capital. On the supply side of this process, financial institutions stepped forward with a vast array of new financial instruments: futures, options, derivatives, hedge funds, etc. The result was skyrocketing financial speculation that has persisted now for decades.

Among orthodox economists there were a few who were concerned early on by this disproportionate growth of finance. In 1984 James Tobin, a former member of Kennedy's Council of Economic Advisers and winner of the Nobel Prize in economics in 1981, delivered a talk "On the Efficiency of the Financial System" in which he concluded by referring to "the casino aspect of our financial markets." As Tobin told his audience:

> I confess to an uneasy Physiocratic suspicion . . . that we are throwing more and more of our resources . . . into financial activities remote from the production of goods and services, into activities that generate high private rewards disproportionate to their social productivity. I suspect that the immense power of the computer is being harnessed to this "paper economy," not to do the same transactions more economically but to balloon the quantity and variety of financial exchanges. For this reason perhaps, high technology has so far yielded disappointing results in economy-wide productivity. I fear that, as Keynes saw even in his day, the advantages of the liquidity and negotiability of financial instruments come at the cost of facilitating nth-degree speculation which is short-sighted and inefficient. . . . I suspect that Keynes was right to suggest that we should provide greater deterrents to transient holdings of financial instruments and larger rewards for long-term investors.[8]

Tobin's point was that capitalism was becoming inefficient by devoting its surplus capital increasingly to speculative, casino-like pursuits, rather than long-term investment in the real economy.[9] In the 1970s he had proposed what subsequently came to be known as the "Tobin tax" on international foreign exchange transactions. This was designed to strengthen investment by shifting the weight of the global economy back from speculative finance to production.

In sharp contrast to those like Tobin who suggested that the rapid growth of finance was having detrimental effects on the real economy, Magdoff and Sweezy, in a 1985 article entitled "The Financial

Explosion," claimed that financialization was functional for capitalism in the context of a tendency to stagnation:

> Does the casino society in fact channel far too much talent and energy into financial shell games. Yes, of course. No sensible person could deny it. Does it do so at the expense of producing real goods and services? Absolutely not. There is no reason whatever to assume that if you could deflate the financial structure, the talent and energy now employed there would move into productive pursuits. They would simply become unemployed and add to the country's already huge reservoir of idle human and material resources. Is the casino society a significant drag on economic growth? Again, absolutely not. What growth the economy has experienced in recent years, apart from that attributable to an unprecedented peacetime military buildup, has been almost entirely due to the financial explosion.[10]

In this view capitalism was undergoing a transformation, represented by the complex, developing relation that had formed between stagnation and financialization. Nearly a decade later in "The Triumph of Financial Capital" Sweezy declared:

> I said that this financial superstructure has been the creation of the last two decades. This means that its emergence was roughly contemporaneous with the return of stagnation in the 1970s. But doesn't this fly in the face of all previous experience? Traditionally financial expansion has gone hand-in-hand with prosperity in the real economy. Is it really possible that this is no longer true, that now in the late twentieth century the opposite is more nearly the case: in other words, that now financial expansion feeds not on a healthy real economy but on a stagnant one?
>
> The answer to this question, I think, is yes it is possible, and it has been happening. And I will add that I am quite convinced that the inverted relation between the financial and the real is the key to understanding the new trends in the world [economy].

In retrospect, it is clear that this "inverted relation" was a built-in possibility for capitalism from the start. But it was one that could materialize only in a definite stage of the development of the system. The abstract possibility lay in the fact, emphasized by both Marx and Keynes, that the capital accumulation process was twofold: involving the ownership of real assets and also the holding of paper claims to those real assets. Under these circumstances the possibility of a contradiction between real accumulation and financial speculation was intrinsic to the system from the beginning.

Although orthodox economists have long assumed that productive investment and financial investment are tied together—working on the simplistic assumption that the saver purchases a financial claim to real assets from the entrepreneur who then uses the money thus acquired to expand production—this has long been known to be false. There is no necessary direct connection between productive investment and the amassing of financial assets. It is thus possible for the two to be "decoupled" to a considerable degree.[11] However, without a mature financial system this contradiction went no further than the speculative bubbles that dot the history of capitalism, normally signaling the end of a boom. Despite presenting serious disruptions, such events had little or no effect on the structure and function of the system as a whole.

It took the rise of monopoly capitalism in the late nineteenth and early twentieth centuries and the development of a market for industrial securities before finance could take center-stage, and before the contradiction between production and finance could mature. In the opening decades of the new regime of monopoly capital, investment banking, which had developed in relation to the railroads, emerged as a financial power center, facilitating massive corporate mergers and the growth of an economy dominated by giant, monopolistic corporations. This was the age of J. P. Morgan. Thorstein Veblen in the United States and Rudolf Hilferding in Austria both independently developed theories of monopoly capital in this period, emphasizing the role of finance capital in particular.

Nevertheless, when the decade of the Great Depression hit, the financial superstructure of the monopoly capitalist economy collapsed, marked by the 1929 stock market crash. Finance capital was greatly diminished in the Depression and played no essential role in the recovery of the real economy. What brought the U.S. economy out of the

Depression was the huge state-directed expansion of military spending during the Second World War.[12]

When Paul Baran and Paul Sweezy wrote *Monopoly Capital* in the early 1960s they emphasized the way in which the state (civilian and military spending), the sales effort, a second great wave of automobilization, and other factors had buoyed the capitalist economy in the golden age of the 1960s, absorbing surplus and lifting the system out of stagnation. They also pointed to the vast amount of surplus that went into FIRE (finance, investment, and real estate), but placed relatively little emphasis on this at the time.

However, with the reemergence of economic stagnation in the 1970s Sweezy, now writing with Magdoff, focused increasingly on the growth of finance. In 1975 in "Banks: Skating on Thin Ice," they argued that "the overextension of debt and the overreach of the banks was exactly what was needed to protect the capitalist system and its profits; to overcome, at least temporarily, its contradictions; and to support the imperialist expansion and wars of the United States."[13]

MONOPOLY-FINANCE CAPITAL

If in the 1970s "the old structure of the economy, consisting of a production system served by a modest financial adjunct" still remained—Sweezy observed in 1995—by the end of the 1980s this "had given way to a new structure in which a greatly expanded financial sector had achieved a high degree of independence and sat on top of the underlying production system."[14] Stagnation and enormous financial speculation emerged as symbiotic aspects of the same deep-seated, irreversible economic impasse.

This symbiosis had three crucial aspects: (1) The stagnation of the underlying economy meant that capitalists were increasingly dependent on the growth of finance to preserve and enlarge their money capital. (2) The financial superstructure of the capitalist economy could not expand entirely independently of its base in the underlying productive economy—hence the bursting of speculative bubbles was a recurrent and growing problem.[15] (3) Financialization, no matter how far it extended, could never overcome stagnation within production.

The role of the capitalist state was transformed to meet the new imperatives of financialization. The state's role as lender of last resort, responsible for providing liquidity at short notice, was fully incorporated into the system. Following the 1987 stock market crash the Federal Reserve adopted an explicit "too big to fail" policy toward the entire equity market, which did not, however, prevent a precipitous decline in the stock market in 2000.[16]

These conditions marked the rise of what we are calling "monopoly-finance capital" in which financialization has become a permanent structural necessity of the stagnation-prone economy.

CLASS AND IMPERIAL IMPLICATIONS

If the roots of financialization are clear from the foregoing, it is also necessary to address the concrete class and imperial implications. Given space limitations we will confine ourselves to eight brief observations.

(1) Financialization can be regarded as an ongoing process transcending particular financial bubbles. If we look at recent financial meltdowns beginning with the stock market crash of 1987, what is remarkable is how little effect they had in arresting or even slowing down the financialization trend. Half the losses in stock market valuation from the Wall Street blowout between March 2000 and October 2002 (measured in terms of the Standard & Poor's 500) had been regained only two years later. While in 1985 U.S. debt was about twice GDP, two decades later U.S. debt had risen to nearly three and a half times the nation's GDP, approaching the $44 trillion GDP of the entire world. The average daily volume of foreign exchange transactions rose from $570 billion in 1989 to $2.7 trillion in 2006. Since 2001 the global credit derivatives market (the global market in credit risk transfer instruments) has grown at a rate of over 100 percent per year. Of relatively little significance at the beginning of the new millennium, the notional value of credit derivatives traded globally ballooned to $26 trillion by the first half of 2006.[17]

(2) Monopoly-finance capital is a qualitatively different phenomenon from what Hilferding and others described as the early-twentieth-century age of "finance capital," rooted especially in the dominance of investment-

banking. Although studies have shown that the profits of financial corporations have grown relative to nonfinancial corporations in the United
States in recent decades, there is no easy divide between the two since
nonfinancial corporations are also heavily involved in capital and money
markets.[18] The great agglomerations of wealth seem to be increasingly
related to finance rather than production, and finance more and more sets
the pace and the rules for the management of the cash flow of nonfinancial firms. Yet, the coalescence of nonfinancial and financial corporations
makes it difficult to see this as constituting a division within capital itself.

(3) Ownership of very substantial financial assets is clearly the main
determinant of membership in the capitalist class. The gap between the
top and the bottom of society in financial wealth and income has now
reached astronomical proportions. In the United States in 2001 the top 1
percent of holders of financial wealth (which excludes equity in owner-
occupied houses) owned more than four times as much as the bottom 80
percent of the population. The nation's richest 1 percent of the population holds $1.9 trillion in stocks, about equal to that of the other 99 per-
cent.[19] The income gap in the United States has widened so much in
recent decades that Federal Reserve Board Chairman Ben S. Bernanke
delivered a speech on February 6, 2007, on "The Level and Distribution
of Economic Well Being," highlighting "a long-term trend toward greater
inequality seen in real wages." As Bernanke stated, "the share of after-tax
income garnered by the households in the top 1 percent of the income
distribution increased from 8 percent in 1979 to 14 percent in 2004." In
September 2006 the richest 60 Americans owned an estimated $630 bil-
lion worth of wealth, up almost 10 percent from the year before.[20]

Recent history suggests that rapid increases in inequality have
become built-in necessities of the monopoly-finance capital phase of the
system. The financial superstructure's demand for new cash infusions to
keep speculative bubbles expanding lest they burst is seemingly endless.
This requires heightened exploitation and a more unequal distribution of
income and wealth, intensifying the overall stagnation problem.

(4) A central aspect of the stagnation-financialization dynamic has
been speculation in housing. This has allowed homeowners to maintain

their lifestyles to a considerable extent despite stagnant real wages by borrowing against growing home equity. As Pollin observed, Magdoff and
Sweezy "recognized before almost anybody the increase in the reliance on
debt by U.S. households [drawing on the expanding equity of their
homes] as a means of maintaining their living standard as their wages
started to stagnate or fall."[21] But low interest rates since the last recession
have encouraged true speculation in housing fueling a housing bubble.
Today the pricking of the housing bubble has become a major source of
instability in the U.S. economy. Consumer debt service ratios have been
rising, while the soaring house values on which consumers have depended to service their debts have disappeared at present. The prices of single-family homes fell in more than half of the country's 149 largest metro-
politan areas in the last quarter of 2006.[22]

So crucial has the housing bubble been as a counter to stagnation and
a basis for financialization, and so closely related is it to the basic well-
being of U.S. households, that the current weakness in the housing market could precipitate both a sharp economic downturn and widespread
financial disarray. Further rises in interest rates have the potential to generate a vicious circle of stagnant or even falling home values and burgeoning consumer debt service ratios leading to a flood of defaults. The fact
that U.S. consumption is the core source of demand for the world economy raises the possibility that this could contribute to a more globalized
crisis.

(5) A thesis currently popular on the left is that financial globalization
has so transformed the world economy that states are no longer important. Rather, as Ignacio Ramonet put it in "Disarming the Market":

> Financial globalization is a law unto itself and it has established a sepa-
> rate supranational state with its own administrative apparatus, its own
> spheres of influence, its own means of action. That is to say, the
> International Monetary Fund (IMF), the World Bank, the Organization
> of Economic Cooperation and Development (OECD) and the World
> Trade Organization (WTO). . . . This artificial world state is a power with
> no base in society. It is answerable instead to the financial markets and
> the mammoth business undertakings that are its masters. The result is

that the real states in the real world are becoming societies with no power base. And it is getting worse all the time. [23]

Such views, however, have little real basis. While the financialization of the world economy is undeniable, to see this as the creation of a new international of capital is to make a huge leap in logic. Global monopoly-finance capitalism remains an unstable and divided system. The IMF, the World Bank, and the WTO (the heir to GATT) do not (even if the OECD were also added in) constitute "a separate supranational state," but are international organizations that came into being in the Bretton Woods System imposed principally by the United States to manage the global system in the interests of international capital following the Second World War. They remain under the control of the leading imperial states and their economic interests. The rules of these institutions are applied asymmetrically—least of all where such rules interfere with U.S. capital, most of all where they further the exploitation of the poorest peoples in the world.

(6) What we have come to call "neoliberalism" can be seen as the ideological counterpart of monopoly-finance capital, as Keynesianism was of the earlier phase of classical monopoly capital. Today's international capital markets place serious limits on state authorities to regulate their economies in such areas as interest-rate levels and capital flows. Hence, the growth of neoliberalism as the hegemonic economic ideology beginning in the Thatcher and Reagan periods reflected to some extent the new imperatives of capital brought on by financial globalization.

(7) The growing financialization of the world economy has resulted in greater imperial penetration into underdeveloped economies and increased financial dependence, marked by policies of neoliberal globalization. One concrete example is Brazil where the first priority of the economy during the last couple of decades under the domination of global monopoly-finance capital has been to attract foreign (primarily portfolio) investment and to pay off external debts to international capital, including the IMF. The result has been better "economic fundamentals" by financial criteria, but accompanied by high interest rates, deindustrialization, slow growth of the economy, and increased vulnerability to the often rapid movements of global finance.[24]

(8) The financialization of capitalism has resulted in a more uncontrollable system. Today the fears of those charged with the responsibility for establishing some modicum of stability in global financial relations are palpable. In the early 2000s in response to the 1997–98 Asian financial crisis, the bursting of the "New Economy" bubble in 2000, and Argentina's default on its foreign debts in 2001, the IMF began publishing a quarterly *Global Financial Stability Report*. One scarcely has to read far in its various issues to get a clear sense of the growing volatility and instability of the system. It is characteristic of speculative bubbles that once they stop expanding they burst. Continual increase of risk and more and more cash infusions into the financial system therefore become stronger imperatives the more fragile the financial structure becomes. Each issue of the *Global Financial Stability Report* is filled with references to the specter of "risk aversion," which is seen as threatening financial markets.

In the September 2006 *Global Financial Stability Report* the IMF executive board directors expressed worries that the rapid growth of hedge funds and credit derivatives could have a systemic impact on financial stability, and that a slowdown of the U.S. economy and a cooling of its housing market could lead to greater "financial turbulence," which could be "amplified in the event of unexpected shocks."[25] The whole context is that of a financialization so out of control that unexpected and severe shocks to the system and resulting financial contagions are looked upon as inevitable. As historian Gabriel Kolko has written, "People who know the most about the world financial system are increasingly worried, and for very good reasons. Dire warnings are coming from the most 'respectable' sources. Reality has gotten out of hand. The demons of greed are loose."[26]

PART TWO

Consequences

5. The Financialization of Capital and the Crisis

April 2008

With the benefit of hindsight, few now doubt that the housing bubble that induced most of the recent growth of the U.S. economy was bound to burst or that a general financial crisis and a global economic slowdown were to be the unavoidable results. Warning signs were evident for years to all of those not taken in by the new financial alchemy of high-risk debt management, and not blinded, as was much of the corporate world, by huge speculative profits. Since the 1960s, *Monthly Review*, first under the editorship of Harry Magdoff and Sweezy and subsequently in the work of the present authors and others, has focused its political-economic analysis on the rapid growth of finance/debt in relation to GDP as the principal counter to the stagnation tendency in the economy. This was not a case of prediction but simply paying attention to the changing nature of the accumulation process in advanced capitalism. Nevertheless, we have long understood that the long-term trajectory of monopoly-finance capital was so unstable that it could only be "solved" ultimately by a severe wiping out of capital. As ever, it remains true today, as Marx said, that "the *real barrier* of capitalist production is *capital itself.*" Nor was there any doubt about what would most likely follow such a collapse if it were to occur: a deeper, longer-lasting condition of stagnation.[1]

As it turned out, the bursting of the U.S. housing bubble set off a chain reaction of stagnant and falling home prices, a flood of defaults, and a global economic crisis due to financial contagion and a drop of U. S. consumption. Since the collapse of the subprime mortgage market in July 2007, financial distress and panic have spread uncontrollably not only across countries but also across financial markets themselves, infecting one sector after another: adjustable-rate mortgages, commercial paper (short-term corporate debt), bond insurers, commercial mortgage lending, corporate bonds, auto loans, credit cards, and student loans.

Banks, hedge funds, and money markets are all under assault. Given the already weak condition of U.S. production, it did not take long for this financial unraveling to be registered in negative numbers in the "real" economy: falling employment, weakening consumption and investment, and decreasing production and profits. Most business and economic analysts now believe that a full-blown recession is ahead both for the United States and the world economy, and may already have begun. "As of right now," former Federal Reserve Board chairman Alan Greenspan stated on February 25, 2008, "U.S. economic growth is zero. We are at stall speed."[2]

What we will argue here is that this is not just another massive credit crunch of the kind so familiar in the history of capitalism, but signals a new phase in the development of the contradictions of the system, which we have labeled "monopoly-finance capital." The bursting of two major financial bubbles in seven years in the citadel of capitalism points to a crisis of financialization, or of the progressive shift in gravity from production to finance that has characterized the economy over the last four decades.

What Paul Sweezy just over a decade ago called "the financialization of the capital accumulation process" has been the main force lifting economic growth since the 1970s.[3] The transformation in the system that this has brought about is reflected in the rapid growth since the 1970s of financial profits as a percent of total profits (see Chart 5.1). The fact that such financialization of capital appears to be taking the form of bigger and bigger bubbles that burst more frequently and with more devastating

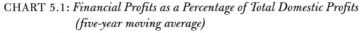

CHART 5.1: *Financial Profits as a Percentage of Total Domestic Profits (five-year moving average)*

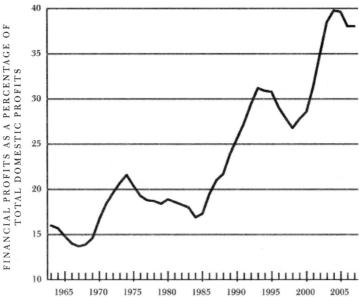

Source: *Economic Report of the President, 2008*, "Corporate Profits by Industry, 1959-2007," Table B-91.

effect, threatening each time a deepening of stagnation—i.e., the condition, endemic to mature capitalism, of slow growth, and rising excess capacity and unemployment/underemployment—is thus a development of major significance.

In order to address this issue we will first examine the evolution of the immediate crisis identified with the bursting of the housing bubble. Only then will we turn to the question of the long-run trend of accumulation, namely the stagnation-financialization dynamic, where the larger historical conditions of the present crisis are to be found.

THE FIVE PHASES OF A BUBBLE

Although the massive stock market decline in 2000 seemed to presage a serious economic decline, business losses were cushioned and wider economic disruptions were curtailed by a real estate bubble—leading to only

a relatively minor recession in 2001. Financial analyst Stephanie Pomboy
at MacroMavens aptly dubbed this in 2002 as "The Great Bubble
Transfer," in which a speculative bubble in the home mortgage market
miraculously compensated for the bursting of the stock market bubble.[4]
Fed by low interest rates and changes in reserve requirements of banks
(which made more funds available) capital flowed massively into the
housing market, mortgage lending skyrocketed, housing prices soared,
and hyperspeculation soon set in.

What occurred followed the basic pattern of speculative bubbles
throughout the history of capitalism, as famously depicted by Charles
Kindleberger in *Manias, Panics, and Crashes*: a novel offering, credit
expansion, speculative mania, distress, and crash/panic.[5]

NOVEL OFFERING

A novel offering may be a new market, a revolutionary new technology, an
innovative product, etc.[6] The novel offering in this case was the "securi-
tization" of mortgage loans through a new financial instrument known as
the collateralized debt obligation (CDO). Since the 1970s banks had
been pooling individual mortgage loans, using the cash flow provided by
these loans to generate residential mortgage-backed securities. These
securitized loans in a later development were themselves repackaged in
the form of CMOs ("Collateralized Mortgage Obligations"). The CMOs
were comprised of what were known as "tranches," or groupings of
income streams from mortgages divided so as to pay off the principal of
each tranche's debt in sequence—the highest tranche first, and so on. In
the 1990s, and especially at the end of the decade, banks began to con-
struct CDOs, which mixed together low-risk, middle-risk, and high-risk
(subprime) mortgages, along with other types of debt.

The tranches now represented risk of default, with the lowest tranche
absorbing all defaults before the next higher tranche, and so on. The
three major credit agencies gave the higher tranches of these new CDOs
investment-grade ratings. (An investment grade bond is one judged likely enough to meet payment obligations that banks are allowed to invest in
them—a bond below investment grade is a junk bond.) The assumption

was that geographical and sector dispersion of the loan portfolio and the "slicing and dicing" of risk would convert all but the very lowest of the tranches of these investment vehicles into safe bets. In many cases the highest (and largest) tranche of such CDOs obtained the best possible rating ("AAA"—equivalent to the rating of the obligations of the U.S. government) through the device of being "insured" against default by a bond-insuring company that itself had been granted AAA ratings. All of this created a vastly expanded market for mortgage lending. This quickly encompassed so-called "subprime" borrowers with poor credit histories and/or low incomes previously outside the mortgage market. And by obtaining high credit ratings for the resulting instruments, the bank creators of these securities obtained the ability to dispose of them readily throughout the new global financial markets.

Crucial to the housing bubble were off-balance-sheet conduits set up by banks, known as structured investment vehicles (SIVs)—themselves virtual banks—designed to hold CDOs. These special entities financed their purchases of CDOs by drawing on the commercial paper market for short-term funds. This meant that they were borrowing short-term funds (through the issue of "asset-backed commercial paper") to invest in long-term securities. In order to reassure investors, "credit default swap" arrangements were made with banks, involving big banks like Bank of America, whereby SIVs (in this case the swap buyers) made quarterly payments in return for banks (the swap sellers) promising to make a large payment if the SIVs found their assets declining and their credit drying up and were forced into default. This along with other factors had the effect of leaving banks potentially exposed to risks that they had supposedly transferred elsewhere.[7]

CREDIT EXPANSION

An expansion of credit—which means people or corporations are taking on more debt—is required to feed any asset price bubble. In the housing bubble extremely low interest rates following the bursting of the stock market bubble and changes in reserve requirements of banks expanded the credit available to borrowers across the board, regardless of their credit history. Beginning in January 2001, the Federal Reserve Board lowered interest rates in twelve successive rate cuts, reducing the key federal funds rate from 6 percent down to a post–Second World War low of 1 percent by June 2003.[8]

In the resulting housing bubble cheap financing expanded the number of mortgage borrowers despite the increasing prices of houses. The combination of extraordinarily low interest rates and longer mortgages resulted in affordable monthly payments even while prices were rapidly increasing. If such monthly payments were still unaffordable—as they often were given that real wages had stagnated for thirty years and entry level jobs rarely paid more than close to the minimum wage—means were devised to lower the initial payments yet further. This often took the form of adjustable rate mortgages with low "teaser" interest rates, which would be reset after a specified introductory period, usually three to five years or less. Paying almost no interest and making no capital payments, new buyers could now "afford" homes at even higher prices.

Unsophisticated home buyers were readily gulled by the overpowering real estate boom euphoria, and easily led to believe that the continual rise in the prices of their homes would allow them to refinance their mortgages when teaser rates expired. Many subprime mortgage loans amounted to 100 percent of the appraised value of the house. The originators of the subprime loans had every incentive to generate and bundle together as many of these loans as possible since the repackaged loans were quickly sold off to others. And, of course, the rapidly inflating home purchase costs covered by these subprime mortgages included a rich rake-off in the form of commissions and fees to a vast predatory swarm of intermediaries in the brokerage and mortgage generating "industry." "The amount of subprime mortgages issued and imbedded in Mortgage Backed Securities shot up from $56 billion in 2000 to $508 billion at the peak in 2005."[9]

SPECULATIVE MANIA

Speculative mania is characterized by a rapid increase in the quantity of debt and an equally rapid decrease in its quality. Heavy borrowing is used to buy up financial assets, not based on the income streams they will generate but merely on the assumption of increasing prices for these assets. This is what economist Hyman Minsky famously called "Ponzi finance" or hyperspeculation.[10] CDOs, with their exposure to subprime mortgages or financial "toxic waste," increasingly took this classic form.

Not just mortgage lenders and subprime borrowers were caught up in the frenzy. A growing crowd of real estate speculators got into the business of buying houses in order to sell them off at higher prices. Many homeowners also began to view the rapid increase in the value of their homes as natural and permanent, and took advantage of low interest rates to refinance and withdraw cash value from their homes. This was a way to maintain or increase consumption levels despite stagnant wages for most workers. At the height of the bubble new mortgage borrowing increased by $1.11 trillion between October and December 2005 alone, bringing outstanding mortgage debt as a whole to $8.66 trillion, equal to 69.4 percent of U.S. GDP.[11]

DISTRESS

Distress marks an abrupt change in the direction of the financial market often resulting from some external event. The housing bubble was first pricked in 2006 due to rising interest rates, which caused a reversal in the direction of housing prices in the hot subprime regions, primarily California, Arizona, and Florida. Borrowers who had been depending on double-digit increases in home prices and very low interest rates to refinance or sell homes before the adjustable rate mortgages were reset were suddenly confronted with falling home prices and mortgage payments that were ratcheting (or would soon ratchet) upwards. Investors began to worry that the cooling down of the housing market in some regions would spread to the mortgage market as a whole and infect the overall economy. As an indicator of such distress, credit debt swaps, designed to protect investors and used to speculate on credit quality, increased globally by 49 percent to cover a notional $42.5 trillion in debt in the first half of 2007.[12]

CRASH AND PANIC

The final stage in a financial bubble is known as crash and panic, marked by a rapid selling off of assets in a "flight to quality" (i.e., liquidity). Cash once again becomes king. The initial crash that shook the market occurred in July 2007 when two Bear Stearns hedge funds that held nearly $10 billion in mortgage-backed securities imploded. One lost 90 percent of its value, while the other melted down completely. As it became apparent that these hedge funds were unable to figure out the actual value of their holdings numerous banks in Europe and Asia as well as the United States, were forced to acknowledge their exposure to toxic subprime mortgages. A severe credit crunch ensued as fear spread among financial institutions, each of which was unsure as to the level of financial toxic waste the other was holding. The seepage of the credit crunch into the commercial paper market cut off the main source of funding for the bank-sponsored SIVs. This brought to the fore the very heavy risk exposure of some of the big banks arising from credit default swaps. A key event was the failure and subsequent bailing out and nationalization of the British mortgage lender Northern Rock, which in September 2007 was the first British bank in over a century to experience a bank run, with customers lining up to withdraw their savings accounts. U.S. bond insurers also began to implode—a development particularly threatening to capital—due to their underwriting of credit-default swaps on mortgage-backed securities.[13]

The financial panic quickly spread around the globe, reflecting the fact that international investors were also heavily tied into speculation on U.S. mortgage-backed securities. Widespread fears emerged that world economic growth would drop to the 2.5 percent or lower level that for economists defines a world recession.[14] Much of the fear that swept through global financial markets was due to a system so complex and opaque that no one knew where the financial toxic waste was buried. This led to a stampede into U.S. Treasury bills and a drastic decrease in lending.

By January 19, 2008, the *Wall Street Journal* openly declared that the financial system had entered "The Panic Stage," referring to Kindleberger's model in *Manias, Panics, and Crashes.* The Federal Reserve Board responded in its lender of last resort function by pouring liquidity back into the system, drastically lowering the federal funds rate from 4.75 percent in September to 3 percent in January with more interest rate cuts expected to come. The federal government stepped in with a $150 billion stimulus package. Nothing, however, has served, as of this writing (in early March 2008), to halt the crisis, which is based in the insolvency of much of the multi-trillion-dollar mortgage market, with new shocks to follow as millions of adjustable rate mortgages see jumps in interest rates. Above all, the end of the housing bubble has undermined the financial condition of already hard-pressed, heavily indebted U.S. consumers, whose purchases equal 72 percent of GDP.

How serious the economic deceleration will be in the end is still unknown. Financial analysts suggest that house prices must fall on average by something like 20–30 percent, and much more in some regions, to get back in line with historical trends.[15] The decline in U.S. housing prices experienced an accelerated decline in the fourth quarter of 2007.[16] That plus the fact that consumers are being hard hit by other problems such as rising fuel and food prices guarantees a serious slowdown. Some observers now refer to a "bubble cycle" and look to another bubble as the only way to avert catastrophe and quickly restore growth to the economy.[17] Others see a period of persistently weak growth.

One thing is certain. Large capitalist interests are relatively well-placed to protect their investments in the downswing through all sorts of hedging arrangements and can often call on the government to bail them out. They also have a myriad of ways of transferring the costs to those lower down on the economic hierarchy. Losses will therefore fall disproportionately on small investors, workers, consumers, and on third world economies. The end result, as in all such episodes in the history of the system, will be increased economic and financial sector concentration on both the national and global scales.

A CRISIS OF FINANCIALIZATION

Little more can be said at the moment about the evolution of the downturn itself, which will still have to work its way through the system. From a long-term historical perspective, however, these events can be seen as symptomatic of a more general crisis of financialization, beyond which lurks the specter of stagnation. It is by exploring these wider and deeper issues rooted in class-based production that we can throw light on the significance of the above developments for capital accumulation and the future of capitalist class society.

Numerous commentators have castigated the U.S. economy for its "monstrous bubble of cheap credit . . . with one bubble begetting another"—in the words of Stephen Roach, chairman of Morgan Stanley Asia. Elsewhere Roach has observed that "America's bubbles have gotten bigger, as have the segments of the real economy they have infected." Household debt has risen to 133 percent of disposable personal income, while the debt of financial corporations has hit the stratosphere, and government and non-financial corporate debt have been steadily increasing.[18] This huge explosion in debt—consumer, corporate, and government—relative to the underlying economy (equal to well over 300 percent of GDP by the housing bubble's peak in 2005) has both lifted the economy and led to growing instability.[19]

Mainstream commentators often treat this as a national neurosis tied to a U.S. addiction to high consumption, high borrowing, and vanishing personal savings, made possible by the infusion of capital from abroad, itself encouraged by the hegemony of the dollar. Radical economists, however, have taken the lead in pointing to a structural transformation in the capital accumulation process itself associated with the decades-long historical process—now commonly called financialization—in which the traditional role of finance as a helpful servant to production has been stood on its head, with finance now dominating over production.

The issue of financialization of the capital accumulation process was underscored a quarter-century ago in *Monthly Review* by Harry Magdoff and Paul Sweezy in an article on "Production and Finance." Starting with a theory (called the "stagnation thesis")[20] that saw financial explosion as a response to the stagnation of the underlying economy, they argued that this helped to "offset the surplus productive capacity of modern industry" both through its direct effect on employment and indirectly through the stimulus to demand created by an appreciation of assets (now referred to as the "wealth effect").[21] But the question naturally arose: Could such a process continue? They answered:

From a structural point of view, i.e., given the far-reaching independence of the financial sector discussed above, financial inflation of this kind can persist indefinitely. But is it not bound to collapse in the face of the stubborn stagnation of the productive sector? Are these two sectors really that independent? Or is what we are talking about merely an inflationary bubble that is bound to burst as many a speculative mania has done in the past history of capitalism?

No assured answer can be given to these questions. But we are inclined to the view that in the present phase of the history of capitalism—barring a by no means improbable shock like the breakdown of the international monetary and banking system—the coexistence of stagnation in the productive sector and inflation in the financial sector can continue for a long time.[22]

At the root of the financialization tendency, Magdoff and Sweezy argued, was the underlying stagnation of the real economy, which was the normal state of modern capitalism. In this view, it was not stagnation that needed explaining so much as periods of rapid growth, such as the 1960s.

Mainstream economists have paid scant attention to the stagnation tendency in the mature economies. In received economic ideology rapid growth is considered to be an intrinsic property of capitalism as a system. Confronted with what looks like the onset of a major economic slowdown we are thus encouraged to see this as a mere cyclical phenomenon— painful, but self-correcting. Sooner rather than later a full recovery will occur and growth will return to its normal fast pace.

There is, however, a radically different economic view, of which Magdoff and Sweezy were among the chief representatives, that suggests that the normal path of the mature capitalist economies, such as those of the United States, the major Western European countries, and Japan, is one of stagnation rather than rapid growth. In this perspective, today's periodic crises, rather than merely constituting temporary interruptions in a process of accelerated advance, point to serious and growing long-term constraints on capital accumulation.

A capitalist economy in order to continue to grow must constantly find new sources of demand for the growing surplus that it generates.

There comes a time, however, in the historical evolution of the economy when much of the investment-seeking surplus generated by the enormous and growing productivity of the system is unable to find sufficient new profitable investment outlets. The reasons for this are complex, having to do with (1) the maturation of economies, in which the basic industrial structure no longer needs to be built up from scratch but simply reproduced (and thus can be normally funded out of depreciation allowances); (2) the absence for long periods of any new technology that generates epoch-making stimulation and transformation of the economy such as with the introduction of the automobile (even the widespread use of computers and the Internet has not had the stimulating effect on the economy of earlier transformative technologies); (3) growing inequality of income and wealth, which limits consumption demand at the bottom of the economy, and tends to reduce investment as unused productive capacity builds up and as the wealthy speculate more with their funds instead of investing in the "real" economy—the goods and services producing sectors; and (4) a process of monopolization (oligopolization), leading to an attenuation of price competition—usually considered to be the main force accounting for the flexibility and dynamism of the system.[23]

Historically, stagnation made its presence felt most dramatically in the Great Depression of the 1930s. It was interrupted by the economic stimulus provided by the Second World War and by the exceptionally favorable conditions immediately after the war in the so-called "Golden Age." But as the favorable conditions waned stagnation resurfaced in the 1970s. Manufacturing capacity utilization began its secular decline that has continued to the present, averaging only 79.8 percent in the 1972–2007 period (as compared to an average of 85 percent in 1960–69). Partly as a result net investment has faltered (see Chart 5.2).[24]

The classical role of net investment (after accounting for replacing depreciated equipment) in the theory of capitalist development is clear. At the firm level, it is only net investment that absorbs investment-seeking surplus corresponding to the undistributed (and untaxed) profits of firms—since the remainder of gross investment is replacement investment covered by capital consumption allowances. As economist Harold Vatter observed in an article entitled "The Atrophy of Net Investment" in 1983,

> On the level of the representative individual enterprise, the withering away of net investment spells approaching termination of the historical and deeply rooted raison d'être of the non-financial firm: accumulation of capital. In consequence, undistributed accounting profits, if not taxed away, would lack the traditional offsets [effective demand in the form of net investment], at least in a closed economy.[25]

It was net investment in the private sector that was once the major driver of the capitalist economy, absorbing a growing economic surplus. It was relatively high net private non-residential fixed investment (togeth-

CHART 5.2: *Net Private Non-Residential Fixed Investment as a Percentage of GDP (five-year moving average)*

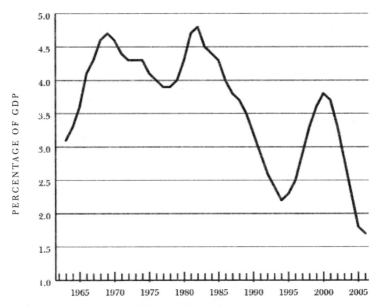

Sources: Bureau of Economic Analysis, National Income and Product Accounts, "Gross and Net Domestic Investments by Major Type, Annual Data 1929–2006," Table 5.2.5; *Economic Report of the President, 2008*, "Gross Domestic Product, 1959–2007," Table B-1.

er with military-oriented government spending) that helped to create and sustain the "Golden Age" of the 1960s. The faltering of such investment (as a percent of GDP) in the early 1970s (with brief exceptions in the late 1970s–early 1980s, and late 1990s), signaled that the economy was unable to absorb all of the investment-seeking surplus that it was generating, and thus marked the onset of deepening stagnation in the real economy of goods and services.

The whole problem has gotten worse over time. Nine out of the ten years with the lowest net non-residential fixed investment as a percentage of GDP over the last half century (up through 2006) were in the 1990s and 2000s. Between 1986 and 2006, in only one year—2000, just before the stock market crash—did the percentage of GDP represented by net private non-residential fixed investment reach the *average* for 1960–79 (4.2 percent). This failure to invest is clearly not due to a lack of investment-seeking surplus. One indicator of this is that corporations are now sitting on a mountain of cash—in excess of $600 billion in corporate savings that have built up at the same time that investment has been declining due to a lack of profitable outlets.[26]

What has mainly kept things from getting worse in the last few decades as a result of the decline of net investment and limits on civilian government spending has been soaring finance. This has provided a considerable outlet for economic surplus in what is called FIRE (finance, insurance, and real estate), employing many new people in this non-productive sector of the economy, while also indirectly stimulating demand through the impact of asset appreciation (the wealth effect).

Aside from finance, the main stimulus to the economy, in recent years, has been military spending. As empire critic Chalmers Johnson noted in the February 2008 *Le Monde Diplomatique*:

> The Department of Defense's planned expenditures for the fiscal year 2008 are larger than all other nations' military budgets combined. The supplementary budget to pay for the current wars in Iraq and Afghanistan, not part of the official defense budget, is itself larger than the combined military budgets of Russia and China. Defense-related spending for fiscal 2008 will exceed $1 trillion for the first time in history. . . .

Leaving out President Bush's two ongoing wars, defense spending has doubled since the mid-1990s. The defense budget for fiscal 2008 is the largest since the second world war.[27]

But, even the stimulus offered by such gargantuan military spending is not enough today to lift U.S. capitalism out of stagnation. Hence, the economy has become more and more dependent on financialization as the key vehicle of growth.

Pointing in 1994 to this dramatically changed economic condition in a talk to Harvard economics graduate students, Sweezy stated:

> In the old days finance was treated as a modest helper of production. It tended to take on a life of its own and generate speculative excesses in the late stages of business cycle expansions. As a rule these episodes were of brief duration and had no lasting effects on the structure and functioning of the economy. In contrast, what has happened in recent years is the growth of a relatively independent financial sector, not in a period of overheating but on the contrary in a period of high-level stagnation (high-level because of the support provided to the economy by the militarily oriented public sector) in which private industry is profitable but lacks incentives to expand, hence stagnation of private real investment. But since corporations and their shareholders are doing well and, as always, are eager to expand their capital, they pour money into the financial markets, which respond by expanding their capacity to handle these growing sums and offering attractive new kinds of financial instruments. Such a process began in the 1970s and really took off in the 1980s. By the end of the decade, the old structure of the economy, consisting of a production system served by a modest financial adjunct, had given way to a new structure in which a greatly expanded financial sector had achieved a high degree of independence and sat on top of the underlying production system. That, in essence, is what we have now.[28]

From this perspective, capitalism in its monopoly-finance capital phase has become increasingly reliant on the ballooning of the credit-debt system in order to escape the worst aspects of stagnation. Moreover, nothing in the financialization process itself offers a way out of this vicious spiral. Today the bursting of two bubbles within seven years in the center of the capitalist system points to a crisis of financialization, behind which lurks deep stagnation, with no visible way out of the trap at present other than the blowing of further bubbles.

IS FINANCIALIZATION THE REAL PROBLEM
OR MERELY A SYMPTOM?

The foregoing argument leads to the conclusion that stagnation generates financialization, which is the main means by which the system continues to limp along at present. But it needs to be noted that recent work by some radical economists in the United States has pointed to the diametrically opposite conclusion: that financialization generates stagnation. In this view it is financialization rather than stagnation that appears to be the real problem.

This can be seen in a November 2007 working paper of the Political Economy Research Institute, written by Thomas Palley, entitled "Financialization: What It Is and Why It Matters." Palley notes that "the era of financialization has been associated with generally tepid economic growth. . . . In all countries except the U.K., average annual growth fell during the era of financialization that set in after 1979. Additionally, growth also appears to show a slowing trend so that growth in the 1980s was higher than in the 1990s, which in turn was higher than in the 2000s." He goes on to observe that "the business cycle generated by financialization may be unstable and end in prolonged stagnation." Nevertheless, the main thrust of Palley's argument is that this "prolonged stagnation" is an outgrowth of financialization rather than the other way around. Thus he contends that such factors as the "wage stagnation and increased income inequality" are "significantly due to changes wrought by financial sector interests." The "new business cycle" dominated by "the cult of debt finance" is said to lead to more volatility arising from financial bubbles. Thus "financialization may render the economy prone to debt-deflation and prolonged recession." Palley calls this argument the "financialization thesis."[29]

There is no doubt that a prolonged deep stagnation could well emerge at the end of a financial bubble, i.e., with the waning of a period of rapid financialization. After all, this is what happened in Japan following the bursting of its real estate-stock market asset bubble in 1990.[30] The analysis that we have presented here, however, would suggest that an economic malaise of this kind is most usefully viewed as a *crisis of financialization* rather than attributable to the negative effects of financialization on the economy, as suggested by Palley. The problem is that the financialization process has stalled and with it the growth it generated.

The point we are making here can be clarified by looking at another (October 2007) working paper (also from the Political Economy Research Institute) by economist Özgür Orhangazi on the subject of "Financialization and Capital Accumulation in the Non-Financial Corporate Sector." Orhangazi argues that "increased financial investment and increased financial profit opportunities crowd out real investment by changing the incentives of the firm managers and directing funds away from real investment." Noting that "the rate of capital accumulation [referring to net non-residential fixed investment by non-financial corporations] has been relatively low in the era of financialization," Orhangazi sees this as due to "increased investment in financial assets," which "can have a 'crowding out' effect on real investment": stagnation then is converted from a cause (as in the stagnation thesis) to an effect (the financialization thesis).[31]

Yet, the idea of the "crowding out" of investment by financial speculation makes little sense, in our view, when placed in the present context of an economy characterized by rising excess capacity and vanishing net investment opportunities. There are just so many profitable outlets for capital in the real economy of goods and services. A very narrow limit exists with regard to the number of profit-generating opportunities associated with the creation of new or expanded automobile or appliance manufacturers, hair salons, fast food outlets, and so on. Under these circumstances of a capital accumulation process that lacks profitable outlets and constantly stalls, the amassing of more and more debt (and the inflation of asset prices that this produces) is a powerful lever, as we have seen, in stimulating growth. Conversely any slowdown in the ballooning of debt threatens that growth. This is not to say that debt should be regarded as a cure-all. To the contrary, for the weak underlying economy of today no amount of debt stimulus is enough. It is in the nature of today's monopoly-finance capital that it "tends to become addicted to debt: more and more is needed just to keep the engine going."[32]

Still, as important as financialization has become in the contemporary economy, this should not blind us to the fact that the real problem lies elsewhere: in the whole system of class exploitation rooted in production. In this sense financialization is merely a way of compensating for the underlying disease affecting capital accumulation itself. As Marx wrote in *Capital*, "The superficiality of political economy shows itself in the fact that it views the expansion and contraction of credit as the cause of the periodic alterations of the industrial cycle, while it is a mere symptom of them." Despite the vast expansion of credit-debt in the capitalism of today, it remains true that the real barrier to capital is capital itself: manifested in the tendency toward overaccumulation of capital.

The well-meaning critique of financialization advanced by Palley, Orhangazi, and others on the left is aimed at the re-regulation of the financial system, and elimination of some of the worst aspects of neoliberalism that have emerged in the age of monopoly-finance capital. The clear intention is to create a new financial architecture that will stabilize the economy and protect wage labor. But if the foregoing argument is correct, such endeavors to re-regulate finance are likely to fail in their main objectives, since any serious attempt to rein in the financial system risks destabilizing the whole regime of accumulation, which constantly needs financialization to soar to ever higher levels.

The only things that could conceivably be done within the system to stabilize the economy, Sweezy stated at Harvard in 1994, would be greatly to expand civilian state spending in ways that genuinely benefited the population; and to carry out a truly radical redistribution of income and wealth of the kind "that Joseph Kennedy, the founder of the Kennedy dynasty" referred to "in the middle of the Great Depression, when things looked bleakest"—indicating "that he would gladly give up half his fortune if he could be sure the other half would be safe." Neither of these radical proposals of course is on the agenda at present, and the nature of capitalism is such that if a crisis ever led to their adoption, every attempt would be made by the vested interests to repeal such measures the moment the crisis had passed.[33]

The hard truth of the matter is that the regime of monopoly-finance capital is designed to benefit a tiny group of oligopolists who dominate both production and finance. A relatively small number of individuals and corporations control huge pools of capital and find no other way to continue to make money on the required scale than through a heavy reliance on finance and speculation. This is a deep-seated contradiction intrinsic to the development of capitalism itself. If the goal is to advance the needs of humanity as a whole, the world will sooner or later have to embrace an alternative system. There is no other way.

6. Back to the Real Economy
December 2008

> But, you may ask, won't the powers that be step into the breach again and abort the crisis before it gets a chance to run its course? Yes, certainly. That, by now, is standard operating procedure, and it cannot be excluded that it will succeed in the same ambiguous sense that it did after the 1987 stock market crash. If so, we will have the whole process to go through again on a more elevated and more precarious level. But sooner or later, next time or further down the road, it will not succeed. . . . We will then be in a new situation as unprecedented as the conditions from which it will have emerged.
>
> —Harry Magdoff and Paul Sweezy (1988)[1]

"The first rule of central banking," economist James K. Galbraith wrote recently, is that "when the ship starts to sink, central bankers must bail like hell."[2] In response to a financial crisis of a magnitude not seen since the Great Depression, the Federal Reserve and other central banks, backed by their treasury departments, have been "bailing like hell" for more than a year. Beginning in July 2007 when the collapse of two Bear Stearns hedge funds that had speculated heavily in mortgage-backed securities signaled the onset of a major credit crunch, the Federal Reserve Board and the U.S. Treasury Department have pulled out all the stops as finance has imploded. They have flooded the financial sector with hundreds of billions of dollars and have promised to pour in trillions more if necessary—operating on a scale and with an array of tools that is unprecedented.

In an act of high drama, Federal Reserve Board Chairman Ben
Bernanke and Secretary of the Treasury Henry Paulson appeared before
Congress on the evening of September 18, 2008, during which the
stunned lawmakers were told, in the words of Senator Christopher Dodd,
"that we're literally days away from a complete meltdown of our financial
system, with all the implications here at home and globally." This was
immediately followed by Paulson's presentation of an emergency plan for
a $700 billion bailout of the financial structure, in which government
funds would be used to buy up virtually worthless mortgage-backed securities (referred to as "toxic waste") held by financial institutions.[3]

The outburst of grassroots anger and dissent, following the Treasury
secretary's proposal, led to an unexpected revolt in the U.S. House of
Representatives, which voted down the bailout plan. Nevertheless, within a few days Paulson's original plan (with some additions intended to
provide political cover for representatives changing their votes) made its
way through Congress. However, once the bailout plan passed financial
panic spread globally with stocks plummeting in every part of the world—
as traders grasped the seriousness of the crisis. The Federal Reserve
responded by literally deluging the economy with money, issuing a state-
ment that it was ready to be the buyer of last resort for the entire commercial paper market (short-term debt issued by corporations), potentially to
the tune of $1.3 trillion.

Yet, despite the attempt to pour money into the system to effect the
resumption of the most basic operations of credit, the economy found itself
in liquidity trap territory, resulting in a hoarding of cash and a cessation of
inter-bank loans as too risky for the banks compared to just holding money.
A liquidity trap threatens when nominal interest rates fall close to zero. The
usual monetary tool of lowering interest rates loses its effectiveness because
of the inability to push interest rates below zero. In this situation the economy is beset by a sharp increase in what Keynes called the "propensity to
hoard" cash or cash-like assets such as Treasury securities.

Fear for the future given what was happening in the deepening crisis
meant that banks and other market participants sought the safety of cash,
so whatever the Fed pumped in failed to stimulate lending. The drive to

liquidity, partly reflected in purchases of Treasuries, pushed the interest rate on Treasuries down to a fraction of 1 percent, i.e., deeper into liquidity trap territory.[4]

Facing what *Business Week* called a "financial ice age," as lending ceased, the financial authorities in the United States and Britain, followed by the G-7 powers as a whole, announced that they would buy ownership shares in the major banks in order to inject capital directly, recapitalizing the banks—a kind of partial nationalization. Meanwhile, they expanded deposit insurance. In the United States the government offered to guarantee $1.5 trillion in new senior debt issued by banks. "All told," as the *New York Times* stated on October 15, 2008, only a month after the Lehman Brothers collapse that set off the banking crisis, "the potential cost to the government of the latest bailout package comes to $2.25 trillion, triple the size of the original $700 billion rescue package, which centered on buying distressed assets from banks."[5] But only a few days later the same paper ratcheted up its estimates of the potential costs of the bailouts overall, declaring: "In theory, the funds committed for everything from the bailouts of Fannie Mae and Freddie Mac and those of Wall Street firm Bear Stearns and the insurer American International Group, to the financial rescue package approved by Congress, to providing guarantees to backstop selected financial markets [such as commercial paper] is a very big number indeed: an estimated $5.1 trillion."[6]

Despite all of this, the financial implosion has continued to widen and deepen, while sharp contractions in the "real economy" are everywhere to be seen. The major U.S. automakers are experiencing serious economic shortfalls, even after Washington agreed in September 2008 to provide the industry with $25 billion in low interest loans. Single-family home construction has fallen to a twenty-six-year low. Consumption is expected to experience record declines. Jobs are rapidly vanishing.[7] Given the severity of the financial and economic shock, there are now widespread fears among those at the center of corporate power that the financial implosion, even if stabilized enough to permit the orderly unwinding and settlement of the multiple insolvencies, will lead to a deep and lasting stagnation, such as hit Japan in the 1990s, or even a new Great Depression.[8]

The financial crisis, as the above suggests, was initially understood as a lack of money or liquidity (the degree to which assets can be traded quickly and readily converted into cash with relatively stable prices). The idea was that this liquidity problem could be solved by pouring more money into financial markets and by lowering interest rates. However, there are a lot of dollars out in the financial world—more now than before—the problem is that those who own the dollars are not willing to lend them to those who may not be able to pay them back, and that's just about everyone who needs the dollars these days. This then is better seen as a solvency crisis in which the balance sheet capital of the U.S. and UK financial institutions—and many others in their sphere of influence—has been wiped out by the declining value of the loans (and securitized loans) they own, their assets.

As an accounting matter, most major U.S. banks by mid-October were insolvent, resulting in a rash of fire-sale mergers, including JPMorgan Chase's purchase of Washington Mutual and Bear Stearns, Bank of America's absorption of Countrywide and Merrill Lynch, and Wells Fargo's acquiring of Wachovia. All of this is creating a more monopolistic banking sector with government support.[9] The direct injection of government capital into the banks in the form of the purchase of shares, together with bank consolidations, will at most buy the necessary time in which the vast mass of questionable loans can be liquidated in orderly fashion, restoring solvency but at a far lower rate of economic activity—that of a serious recession or depression.

In this worsening crisis, no sooner is one hole patched than a number of others appear. The full extent of the loss in value of securitized mortgage, consumer and corporate debts, and the various instruments that attempted to combine such debts with forms of insurance against their default (such as the "synthetic collateralized debt obligations," which have credit-debt swaps "packaged in" with the CDOs), is still unknown. Key categories of such financial instruments have been revalued recently down to 10 to 20 percent in the course of the Lehman Brothers bankruptcy and the takeover of Merrill Lynch.[10] As sharp cuts in the value of such assets are applied across the board, the equity base of financial institutions vanishes along with trust in their solvency. Hence, banks are now doing what John Maynard Keynes said they would in such circumstances: hoarding cash.[11] Underlying all of this is the deteriorating economic condition of households at the base of the economy, impaired by decades of frozen real wages and growing consumer debt.

"It" and the Lender of Last Resort

To understand the full historical significance of these developments it is necessary to look at what is known as the "lender of last resort" function of the U.S. and other capitalist governments. This has now taken the form of offering liquidity to the financial system in a crisis, followed by directly injecting capital into such institutions and finally, if needed, outright nationalizations. It is this commitment by the state to be the lender of last resort that over the years has ultimately imparted confidence in the system—despite the fact that the financial superstructure of the capitalist economy has far outgrown its base in what economists call the "real" economy of goods and services. Nothing therefore is more frightening to capital than the appearance of the Federal Reserve and other central banks doing everything they can to bail out the system and failing to prevent it from sinking further—something previously viewed as unthinkable. Although the Federal Reserve and the U.S. Treasury have been intervening massively, the full dimensions of the crisis still seem to elude them.

Some have called this a "Minsky moment." In 1982, economist Hyman Minsky, famous for his financial instability hypothesis, asked the critical question: "Can 'It'—a Great Depression—happen again?" There were, as he pointed out, no easy answers to this question. For Minsky the key issue was whether a financial meltdown could overwhelm a real economy already in trouble—as in the Great Depression. The inherently unstable financial system had grown in scale over the decades, but so had government and its capacity to serve as a lender of last resort. "The processes which make for financial instability," Minsky observed, "are an inescapable part of any decentralized capitalist economy—i.e., capitalism is inherently flawed—but financial instability need not lead to a great depression; 'It' *need not* happen" (italics added).[12]

Implicit in this, however, was the view that "It" *could* still happen again—if only because the possibility of financial explosion and growing instability could conceivably outgrow the government's capacity to respond—or to respond quickly and decisively enough. Theoretically, the capitalist state, particularly that of the United States, which controls what amounts to a surrogate world currency, has the capacity to avert such a dangerous crisis. The chief worry is a massive "debt-deflation" (a phenomenon explained by economist Irving Fisher during the Great Depression) as exhibited not only by the experience of the 1930s but also Japan in the 1990s. In this situation, as Fisher wrote in 1933, "deflation caused by the debt reacts on the debt. Each dollar of debt still unpaid becomes a bigger dollar, and if the over-indebtedness with which we started was great enough, the liquidation of debt cannot keep up with the fall of prices which it causes." Put differently, prices fall as debtors sell assets to pay their debts, and as prices fall the remaining debts must be repaid in dollars more valuable than the ones borrowed, causing more defaults, leading to yet lower prices, and thus a deflationary spiral.[13]

The economy is still not in this dire situation, but the specter looms. As Paul Asworth, chief U.S. economist at Capital Economics, stated in mid-October 2008, "With the unemployment rate rising rapidly and capital markets in turmoil, pretty much everything points toward deflation. The only thing you can hope is that the prompt action from policy makers can maybe head this off first." "The rich world's economies," the *Economist* magazine warned in early October, "are already suffering from a mild case of this 'debt-deflation.' The combination of falling house prices and credit contraction is forcing debtors to cut spending and sell assets, which in turn pushes house prices and other asset markets down further. . . . A general fall in consumer prices would make matters even worse."[14]

The very thought of such events recurring in the U.S. economy today was supposed to be blocked by the lender of last resort function, based on the view that the problem was primarily monetary and could always be solved by monetary means by flooding the economy with liquidity at the least hint of danger. Thus Federal Reserve Board Chairman Ben

Bernanke gave a talk in 2002 (as a Federal Reserve governor) significantly entitled "Deflation: Making Sure 'It' Doesn't Happen Here." In it he contended that there were ample ways of ensuring that "It" would not happen today, despite increasing financial instability:

> The U.S. government has a technology, called a printing press (or, today, its electronic equivalent) that allows it to produce as many U.S. dollars as it wishes at essentially no cost. By increasing the number of U.S. dollars in circulation, or even by credibly threatening to do so, the U.S. government can also reduce the value of a dollar in terms of goods and services, which is equivalent to raising the prices in dollars of those goods and services. We conclude that, under a paper-money system, a determined government can always generate higher spending and hence positive inflation.
>
> Of course, the U.S. government is not going to print money and distribute it willy-nilly (although as we will see later, there are practical policies that approximate this behavior). Normally, money is injected into the economy through asset purchases by the Federal Reserve. To stimulate aggregate spending when short-term interest rates have reached zero, the Fed must expand the scale of its asset purchases or, possibly, expand the menu of assets that it buys. Alternatively, the Fed, could find other ways of injecting money into the system—for example, by making low-interest-rate loans to banks or cooperating with fiscal authorities. [15]

In the same talk, Bernanke suggested that "a money-financed tax cut," aimed at avoiding deflation in such circumstances, was "essentially equivalent to Milton Friedman's famous 'helicopter drop' of money"—a stance that earned him the nickname "Helicopter Ben."[16]

An academic economist who made his reputation through studies of the Great Depression, Bernanke was a product of the view propounded most influentially by Milton Friedman and Anna Schwartz in their famous work, *A Monetary History of the United States, 1867–1960*, that the source of the Great Depression was monetary and could have been combated almost exclusively in monetary terms. The failure to open the monetary floodgates at the outset, according to Friedman and Schwartz, was the principal reason that the economic downturn was so severe.[17]

Bernanke strongly opposed earlier conceptions of the Depression that
saw it as based in the structural weaknesses of the "real" economy and the
underlying accumulation process. Speaking on the seventy-fifth anniversary of the 1929 stock market crash, he stated:

> During the Depression itself, and in several decades following, most
> economists argued that monetary factors were not an important cause of
> the Depression. For example, many observers pointed to the fact that
> nominal interest rates were close to zero during much of the Depression,
> concluding that monetary policy had been about as easy as possible yet
> had produced no tangible benefit to the economy. The attempt to use
> monetary policy to extricate an economy from a deep depression was
> often compared to "pushing on a string."
>
> During the first decades after the Depression, most economists looked
> to developments on the real side of the economy for explanations, rather
> than to monetary factors. Some argued, for example, that overinvestment
> and overbuilding had taken place during the ebullient 1920s, leading to
> a crash when the returns on those investments proved to be less than
> expected. Another once-popular theory was that a chronic problem of
> "under-consumption"—the inability of households to purchase enough
> goods and services to utilize the economy's productive capacity—had
> precipitated the slump.[18]

Bernanke's answer to all of this was strongly to reassert that monetary
factors virtually alone precipitated (and explained) the Great Depression,
and were the key, indeed almost the sole, means of fighting debt-deflation.
The trends in the real economy, such as the emergence of excess capacity in industry, need hardly be addressed at all. At most it was a deflationary threat to be countered by reflation.[19] Nor, as he argued elsewhere, was
it necessary to explore Minsky's contention that the financial system of
the capitalist economy was inherently unstable, since this analysis
depended on the economic irrationality associated with speculative
manias, and thus departed from the formal "rational economic behavior"
model of neoclassical economics.[20] Bernanke concluded a talk commem-
orating Friedman's ninetieth birthday in 2002 with the words: "I would
like to say to Milton and Anna: Regarding the Great Depression. You're

right, we did it. We're very sorry. But thanks to you, we won't do it again."[21] "It" of course was the Great Depression.

Following the 2000 stock market crash a debate arose in central bank circles about whether "preemptive attacks" should be made against future asset bubbles to prevent such economic catastrophes. Bernanke, representing the reigning economic orthodoxy, led the way in arguing that this should not be attempted, since it was difficult to know whether a bubble was actually a bubble (that is, whether financial expansion was justified by economic fundamentals or new business models or not). In addition, to prick a bubble was to invite disaster, as in the attempts by the Federal Reserve Board to do this in the late 1920s, leading (according to the monetarist interpretation) to the bank failures and the Great Depression. He concluded: "monetary policy cannot be directed finely enough to guide asset prices without risking severe collateral damage to the economy. . . . Although eliminating volatility from the economy and the financial markets will never be possible, we should be able to moderate it without sacrificing the enormous strengths of our free-market system." In short, Bernanke argued, no doubt with some justification given the nature of the system, that the best the Federal Reserve Board could do in face of a major bubble was to restrict itself primarily to its lender of last resort function.[22]

At the very peak of the housing bubble, Bernanke, then chairman of Bush's Council of Economic Advisors, declared with eyes wide shut: "House prices have risen by nearly 25 percent over the past two years. Although speculative activity has increased in some areas, at a national level these price increases largely reflect strong economic fundamentals, including robust growth in jobs and incomes, low mortgage rates, steady rates of household formation, and factors that limit the expansion of housing supply in some areas."[23] Ironically, it was these views that led to the appointment of Bernanke as Federal Reserve Board chairman (replacing Alan Greenspan) in early 2006.

The housing bubble began to deflate in early 2006 at the same time that the Fed was raising interest rates in an attempt to contain inflation. The result was a collapse of the housing sector and mortgage-backed securities. Confronted with a major financial crisis beginning in 2007, Bernanke as Fed chairman put the printing press into full operation, flooding the nation and the world with dollars, and soon found to his dismay that he had been "pushing on a string." No amount of liquidity infusions were able to overcome the insolvency in which financial institutions were mired. Unable to make good on their current financial claims—were they compelled to do so—banks refused to renew loans as they came due and hoarded available cash rather than lending and leveraging the system back up. The financial crisis soon became so universal that the risks of lending money skyrocketed, given that many previously creditworthy borrowers were now quite possibly on the verge of insolvency. In a liquidity trap, as Keynes taught, running the printing presses simply adds to the hoarding of money but not to new loans and spending.

However, the real root of the financial bust, we shall see, went much deeper: the stagnation of production and investment.

FROM FINANCIAL EXPLOSION
TO FINANCIAL IMPLOSION

Our argument in a nutshell is that both the financial explosion in recent decades and the financial implosion now taking place are to be explained mainly in reference to stagnation tendencies within the underlying economy. A number of other explanations for the current crisis (most of them focusing on the proximate causes) have been given by economists and media pundits. These include the lessening of regulations on the financial system; the very low interest rates introduced by the Fed to counter the effects of the 2000 crash of the "New Economy" stock bubble, leading to the housing bubble; and the selling of large amounts of "sub-prime" mortgages to many people who could not afford to purchase a house and/or did not fully understand the terms of the mortgages.

Much attention has rightly been paid to the techniques whereby mortgages were packaged together and then "sliced and diced" and sold to institutional investors around the world. Outright fraud may also have been involved in some of the financial shenanigans. The falling home values following the bursting of the housing bubble and the inability of many subprime mortgage holders to continue to make their monthly payments, together with the resulting foreclosures, was certainly the straw that broke the camel's back, leading to this catastrophic system failure. And few would doubt today that it was all made worse by the deregulation fervor avidly promoted by the financial firms, which left them with fewer defenses when things went wrong.

Nevertheless, the root problem went much deeper, and was to be found in a real economy experiencing slower growth, giving rise to financial explosion as capital sought to "leverage" its way out of the problem by expanding debt and gaining speculative profits. The extent to which debt has shot up in relation to GDP over the last four decades can be seen in Table 6.1. As these figures suggest, the most remarkable feature in the development of capitalism during this period has been the ballooning of debt.

TABLE 6.1: *Domestic Debt and GDP* (trillions of dollars)*

			DEBT BY SECTOR			
	Gross Domestic Product	**Total Debt**	*Household*	*Financial Firm*	*Non-Fin'l Business*	*Gov't (local, state & federal)*
1970	**1.0**	**1.5**	0.5	0.1	0.5	0.4
1980	**2.7**	**4.5**	1.4	0.6	1.5	1.1
1990	**5.8**	**13.5**	3.6	2.6	3.7	3.5
2000	**9.8**	**26.3**	7.0	8.1	6.6	4.6
2007	**13.8**	**47.7**	13.8	16.0	10.6	7.3

*The federal part of local, state, and federal debt includes only that portion held by the public. The total debt in 2007 when the federal debt held by federal agencies is added is $51.5 trillion.

Sources: Federal Reserve, Flow of Funds Accounts of the United States, "Credit Market Debt Outstanding," Table L.1; *Economic Report of the President, 2008*, "Gross Domestic Product, 1959-2007," Table B-1.

This phenomenon is further illustrated in Chart 6.1 showing the skyrocketing of private debt relative to national income from the 1960s to the present. Financial sector debt as a percentage of GDP first lifted off the ground in the 1960s and 1970s, accelerated beginning in the 1980s, and rocketed up after the mid 1990s. Household debt as a percentage of GDP rose strongly beginning in the 1980s and then increased even faster in the late 1990s. Non-financial business debt in relation to national income also climbed over the period, if less spectacularly. The overall effect has been a massive increase in private debt relative to national income. The problem is further compounded if government debt (local, state, and federal) is added in. When all sectors are included, the total debt as a percentage of GDP rose from 151 percent in 1959 to an astronomical 373 percent in 2007!

This rise in the cumulative debt load as a percentage of GDP greatly stimulated the economy, particularly in the financial sector, feeding enormous financial profits and marking the growing financialization of capitalism (the shift in gravity from production to finance within the economy as a whole). The profit picture, associated with this accelerating financialization, is shown is Chart 6.2, which provides a time series index (1970 = 100) of U.S. financial vs. non-financial profits and the GDP. Beginning in 1970, financial and non-financial profits tended to increase at the same

CHART 6.1: *Private Debt as a Percent of GDP*

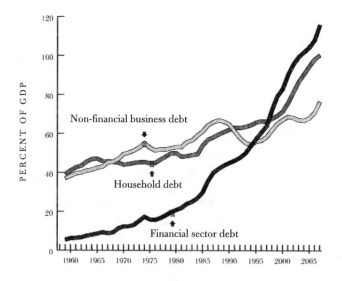

Sources: Same as Table 6.1.

rate as the GDP. However, in the late 1990s, finance seemed to take on a life of its own with the profits of U.S. financial corporations (and to a lesser extent non-financial corporate profits too) heading off into the stratosphere, seemingly unrelated to growth of national income, which was relatively stagnant. Corporations playing in what had become a giant casino took on more and more leveraging—that is, they often bet thirty or more borrowed dollars for every dollar of their own that was used. This helps to explain the extraordinarily high profits they were able to earn as long as their bets were successful. The growth of finance was of course not restricted simply to the United States but was a global phenomenon with speculative claims to wealth far overshadowing global production, and with the same essential contradiction cutting across the entire advanced capitalist world and "emerging" economies.

Already by the late 1980s the seriousness of the situation was becoming clear to those not wedded to established ways of thinking. Looking at this condition in 1988 on the anniversary of the 1987 stock market crash,

CHART 6.2: *Growth of Financial and Non-Financial Profits Relative to GDP (1970 = 100)*

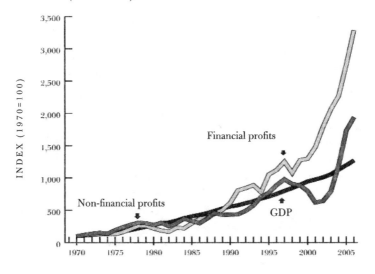

Sources: Calculated from *Economic Report of the President, 2008*, "Corporate profits by industry, 1959-2007," Table B-91, and "Gross domestic product, 1959-2007," Table B-1.

Monthly Review editors Harry Magdoff and Paul Sweezy contended that sooner or later—no one could predict when or exactly how—a major crisis of the financial system that overpowered the lender of last resort function was likely to occur. This was simply because the whole precarious financial superstructure would have by then grown to such a scale that the means of governmental authorities, though massive, would no longer be sufficient to keep back the avalanche, especially if they failed to act quickly and decisively enough. As they put it, the next time around it was quite possible that the rescue effort would "succeed in the same ambiguous sense that it did after the 1987 stock market crash. If so, we will have the whole process to go through again on a more elevated and precarious level. But sooner or later, next time or further down the road, it will not succeed," generating a severe crisis of the economy.

As an example of a financial avalanche waiting to happen, they pointed to the "high flying Tokyo stock market," as a possible prelude to a major financial implosion and a deep stagnation to follow—a reality that was to materialize soon after, resulting in Japan's financial crisis and "Great Stagnation" of the 1990s. Asset values (both in the stock market and real estate) fell by an amount equivalent to more than two years of GDP. As interest rates zeroed out and debt-deflation took over, Japan was stuck in a classic liquidity trap with no ready way of restarting an economy already deeply mired in overcapacity in the productive economy.[24]

"In today's world ruled by finance," Magdoff and Sweezy had written in 1987 in the immediate aftermath of the U.S. stock market crash:

> the underlying growth of surplus value falls increasingly short of the rate of accumulation of money capital. In the absence of a base in surplus value, the money capital amassed becomes more and more nominal, indeed fictitious. It comes from the sale and purchase of paper assets, and is based on the assumption that asset values will be continuously inflated. What we have, in other words, is ongoing speculation grounded in the belief that, despite fluctuations in price, asset values will forever go only one way—upward! Against this background, the October [1987] stock market crash assumes a far-reaching significance. By demonstrating

the fallacy of an unending upward movement in asset values, it exposes the irrational kernel of today's economy.[25]

These contradictions, associated with speculative bubbles, have of course to some extent been endemic to capitalism throughout its history. However, in the post–Second World War era, as Magdoff and Sweezy, in line with Minsky, argued, the debt overhang became larger and larger, pointing to the growth of a problem that was cumulative and increasingly dangerous. In *The End of Prosperity* Magdoff and Sweezy wrote: "In the absence of a severe depression during which debts are forcefully wiped out or drastically reduced, government rescue measures to prevent collapse of the financial system merely lay the groundwork for still more layers of debt and additional strains during the next economic advance." As Minsky put it, "Without a crisis and a debt-deflation process to offset beliefs in the success of speculative ventures, both an upward bias to prices and ever-higher financial layering are induced."[26]

To the extent that mainstream economists and business analysts themselves were momentarily drawn to such inconvenient questions, they were quickly cast aside. Although the spectacular growth of finance could not help but create jitters from time to time—for example, Alan Greenspan's famous reference to "irrational exuberance"—the prevailing assumption, promoted by Greenspan himself, was that the growth of debt and speculation represented a new era of financial market innovation, i.e., a sustainable structural change in the business model associated with revolutionary new risk management techniques. Greenspan was so enamored of the "New Economy" made possible by financialization that he noted in 2004: "Not only have individual financial institutions become less vulnerable to shocks from underlying risk factors, but also the financial system as a whole has become more resilient."[27]

It was only with the onset of the financial crisis in 2007 and its persistence into 2008 that we find financial analysts in surprising places openly taking on the contrary view. Thus as Manas Chakravarty, an economic columnist for India's investor Web site, Livemint.com (partnered with the *Wall Street Journal*), observed on September 17, 2008, in the context of the Wall Street meltdown,

American economist Paul Sweezy pointed out long ago that stagnation and enormous financial speculation emerged as symbiotic aspects of the same deep-seated, irreversible economic impasse. He said the stagnation of the underlying economy meant that business was increasingly dependent on the growth of finance to preserve and enlarge its money capital and that the financial superstructure of the economy could not expand entirely independently of its base in the underlying productive economy. With remarkable prescience, Sweezy said the bursting of speculative bubbles would, therefore, be a recurring and growing problem.[28]

Of course, Paul Baran and Sweezy in *Monopoly Capital,* and later on Magdoff and Sweezy in *Monthly Review,* had pointed to other forms of absorption of surplus such as government spending (particularly military spending), the sales effort, the stimulus provided by new innovations, etc.[29] But all of these, although important, had proven insufficient to maintain the economy at anything like full employment, and by the 1970s the system was mired in deepening stagnation (or stagflation). It was financialization—and the growth of debt that it actively promoted—which was to emerge as the quantitatively most important stimulus to demand. But it pointed unavoidably to a day of financial reckoning and cascading defaults.

Indeed, some mainstream analysts, under the pressure of events, were forced to acknowledge by summer 2008 that a massive devaluation of the system might prove inevitable. Jim Reid, the Deutsche Bank's head of credit research, examining the kind of relationship between financial profits and GDP exhibited in Chart 6.2, issued an analysis called "A Trillion-Dollar Mean Reversion?," in which he argued that:

> U.S. financial profits have deviated from the mean over the past decade on a cumulative basis. . . . The U.S. financial sector has made around 1.2 trillion ($1,200bn) of "excess" profits in the last decade relative to nominal GDP. . . . So mean reversion [the theory that returns in financial markets over time "revert" to a long-term mean projection, or trendline] would suggest that $1.2 trillion of profits need to be wiped out before the U.S. financial sector can be cleansed of the excesses of the last decade. . . . Given that . . . Bloomberg reports that $184bn has been writ-

ten down by U.S. financials so far in this crisis, if one believes that the size of the financial sector should shrink to levels seen a decade ago then one could come to the conclusion that there is another trillion dollars of value destruction to go in the sector before we're back to the long-run trend in financial profits. A scary thought and one that if correct will lead to a long period of constant intervention by the authorities in an attempt to arrest this potential destruction. Finding the appropriate size of the financial sector in the "new world" will be key to how much profit destruction there needs to be in the sector going forward.

The idea of a mean reversion of financial profits to their long-term trend line in the economy as a whole was merely meant to be suggestive of the extent of the impending change, since Reid accepted the possibility that structural "real world" reasons exist to explain the relative weight of finance—though none he was yet ready to accept. As he acknowledged, "calculating the 'natural' appropriate size for the financial sector relative to the rest of the economy is a phenomenally difficult conundrum." Indeed, it was to be doubted that a "natural" level actually existed. But the point that a massive "profit destruction" was likely to occur before the system could get going again, and that this explained the "long period of constant intervention by the authorities in an attempt to arrest this potential destruction," highlighted the fact that the crisis was far more severe than then widely supposed—something that became apparent soon after.[30]

What such thinking suggested, in line with what Magdoff and Sweezy had argued in the closing decades of the twentieth century, was that the autonomy of finance from the underlying economy, associated with the financialization process, was more relative than absolute, and that ultimately a major economic downturn—more than the mere bursting of one bubble and the inflating of another—was necessary. This was likely to be more devastating the longer the system put it off. In the meantime, as Magdoff and Sweezy had pointed out, financialization might go on for quite a while. And indeed there was no other answer for the system.

BACK TO THE REAL ECONOMY:
THE STAGNATION PROBLEM

Paul Baran, Paul Sweezy, and Harry Magdoff argued indefatigably from
the 1960s to the 1990s (most notably in *Monopoly Capital*) that stagnation was the *normal state* of the monopoly-capitalist economy, barring
special historical factors. The prosperity that characterized the economy
in the 1950s and '60s, they insisted, was attributable to such temporary
historical factors as: (1) the buildup of consumer savings during the war;
(2) a second great wave of automobilization in the United States (including the expansion of the glass, steel, and rubber industries, the construction of the interstate highway system, and the development of suburbia);
(3) the rebuilding of the European and the Japanese economies devastat-
ed by the war; (4) the Cold War arms race (and two regional wars in Asia);
(5) the growth of the sales effort marked by the rise of Madison Avenue;
(6) the expansion of FIRE (finance, insurance, and real estate); and (7)
the preeminence of the dollar as the hegemonic currency. Once the
extraordinary stimulus from these factors waned, the economy began to
subside back into stagnation: slow growth and rising excess capacity and
unemployment/underemployment. In the end, it was military spending
and the explosion of debt and speculation that constituted the main stimuli keeping the economy out of the doldrums. These were not sufficient,
however, to prevent the reappearance of stagnation tendencies altogether,
and the problem got worse with time.[31]

The reality of creeping stagnation can be seen in Table 6.2, which
shows the real growth rates of the U.S. economy decade by decade over the
last eight decades. The low growth rate in the 1930s reflected the deep stagnation of the Great Depression. This was followed by the extraordinary rise
of the U.S. economy in the 1940s under the impact of the Second World
War. During the years 1950–69, now often referred to as an economic
"Golden Age," the United States, propelled by the set of special historical
factors referred to above, was able to achieve strong growth in a "peace-
time" economy. This, however, proved to be all too temporary. The sharp
drop-off in growth rates in the 1970s and thereafter points to a persistent
tendency toward slower expansion in the economy, as the main forces

pushing up growth rates in the
1950s and '60s waned, preventing
the economy from returning to its
former prosperity. In subsequent
decades, rather than recovering its
former trend rate of growth, the
economy slowly subsided.

It was the reality of economic
stagnation beginning in the 1970s,
as heterodox economists Riccardo
Bellofiore and Joseph Halevi have
recently emphasized, that led to the
emergence of "the new financialized
capitalist regime," a kind of "para-
doxical *financial Keynesianism*"
whereby demand in the economy
was stimulated primarily "thanks to

TABLE 6.2: *Growth in Real GDP 1930–2007*

	Average Annual Percent
1930s	1.3
1940s	5.9
1950s	4.1
1960s	4.4
1970s	3.3
1980s	3.1
1990s	3.1
2000–2007	2.6

Source: Bureau of Economic Analysis, National Income and Products Accounts, "Percent Change from Preceding Period in Real Gross Domestic Product," Table 1.1.1.

asset-bubbles." Moreover, it was the leading role of the United States in generating such bubbles—despite (and also because of) the weakening of capital accumulation proper—together with the dollar's reserve currency status, that made U.S. monopoly-finance capital the "catalyst of world effective demand," beginning in the 1980s.[32] But such a financialized growth pattern was unable to produce rapid economic advance for any length of time, and was unsustainable, leading to bigger bubbles that peri- odically burst, bringing stagnation more and more to the surface.

A key element in explaining this whole dynamic is to be found in the falling ratio of wages and salaries as a percentage of national income in the United States. Stagnation in the 1970s led capital to launch an accelerat- ed class war against workers to raise profits by pushing labor costs down. The result was decades of increasing inequality.[33] Chart 6.3 shows a sharp decline in the share of wages and salaries in GDP between the late 1960s and the present. This reflected the fact that real wages of private nonagricultural workers in the United States (in 1982 dollars) peaked in 1972 at $8.99 per hour, and by 2006 had fallen to $8.24 (equivalent to the real hourly wage rate in 1967), despite the enormous growth in pro-ductivity and profits over the past few decades.[34]

This was part of a massive redistribution of income and wealth to the top. Over the years 1950 to 1970, for each additional dollar made by those in the bottom 90 percent of income earners, those in the top 0.01 percent received an additional $162. In contrast, from 1990 to 2002, for each added dollar made by those in the bottom 90 percent, those in the uppermost 0.01 percent (today around 14,000 households) made an additional $18,000. In the United States the top 1 percent of wealth hold-ers in 2001 together owned more than twice as much as the bottom 80 percent of the population. If this were measured simply in terms of finan-cial wealth, i.e., excluding equity in owner-occupied housing, the top 1 percent owned more than four times the bottom 80 percent. Between 1983 and 2001, the top 1 percent grabbed 28 percent of the rise in national income, 33 percent of the total gain in net worth, and 52 percent of the overall growth in financial worth.[35]

CHART 6.3: *Wage and Salary Disbursements as a Percentage of GDP*

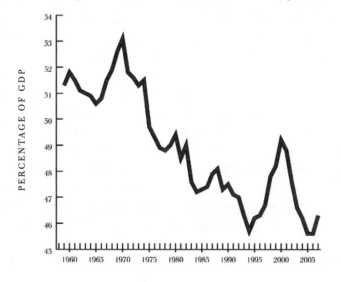

Sources: *Economic Report of the President, 2008*, "Gross Domestic Product, 1959-2007," Table B-1 and "Sources of personal income, 1959–2007," Table B-29.

The truly remarkable fact under these circumstances was that household consumption continued to rise from a little over 60 percent of GDP in the early 1960s to around 70 percent in 2007. This was only possible because of more two-earner households (as women entered the labor force in greater numbers), people working longer hours and filling multiple jobs, and a constant ratcheting up of consumer debt. Household debt was spurred, particularly in the later stages of the housing bubble, by a dramatic rise in housing prices, allowing consumers to borrow more against their increased equity (the so-called housing "wealth effect")—a process that came to a sudden end when the bubble popped, and housing prices started to fall. As Chart 6.1 shows, household debt increased from about 40 percent of GDP in 1960 to 100 percent of GDP in 2007, with an especially sharp increase starting in the late 1990s.[36]

This growth of consumption, based in the expansion of household debt, was to prove to be the Achilles' heel of the economy. The housing bubble was based on a sharp increase in household mortgage-based debt, while real wages had been essentially frozen for decades. The resulting defaults among marginal new owners led to a fall in house prices. This led to an ever increasing number of owners owing more on their houses than they were worth, creating more defaults and a further fall in house prices. Banks seeking to bolster their balance sheets began to hold back on new extensions of credit card debt. Consumption fell, jobs were lost, capital spending was put off, and a downward spiral of unknown duration began.

During the last thirty years or so the economic surplus controlled by corporations, and in the hands of institutional investors, such as insurance companies and pension funds, has poured in an ever increasing flow into an exotic array of financial instruments. Little of the vast economic surplus was used to expand investment, which remained in a state of simple reproduction, geared to mere replacement (albeit with new, enhanced technology), as opposed to expanded reproduction. With corporations unable to find the demand for their output—a reality reflected in the long-run decline of capacity utilization in industry (see Chart 6.4)—and therefore confronted with a dearth of profitable investment opportunities, the process of net capital formation became more and more problematic.

Hence, profits were increasingly directed away from investment in the expansion of productive capacity and toward financial speculation, while the financial sector seemed to generate unlimited types of financial products designed to make use of this money capital. (The same phenomenon existed globally, causing Bernanke to refer in 2005 to a "global savings glut," with enormous amounts of investment-seeking capital circling the world and increasingly drawn to the United States because of its leading role in financialization.)[37] The consequences of this can be seen in Chart 6.5, showing the dramatic decoupling of profits from net investment as percentages of GDP in recent years, with net private nonresidential fixed investment as a share of national income falling significantly over the period, even while profits as a share of GDP approached a level not seen since the late 1960s/early 1970s. This marked, in Marx's terms, a shift from the

CHART 6.4: *Percent Utilization of Industrial Capacity*

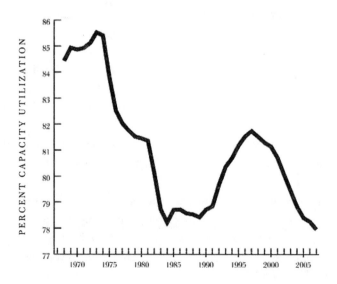

Source: *Economic Report of the President, 2008,* "Capacity utilization rates, 1959–2007," Table B-54.

"general formula for capital" M(oney)–C(commodity)–M´ (original money plus surplus value), in which commodities were central to the production of profits—to a system increasingly geared to the circuit of money capital alone, M–M´, in which money simply begets more money with no relation to production.

Since financialization can be viewed as the response of capital to the stagnation tendency in the real economy, a crisis of financialization inevitably means a resurfacing of the underlying stagnation endemic to the advanced capitalist economy. The deleveraging of the enormous debt built up during recent decades is now contributing to a deep crisis. Moreover, with financialization in crisis there is no other visible way out for monopoly-finance capital. The prognosis then is that the economy, even after the immediate devaluation crisis is stabilized, will at best be characterized for some time by minimal growth and by high unemployment, underemployment, and excess capacity.

CHART 6.5: *Profits and Net Investment as a Percentage of GDP, 1960 to Present*

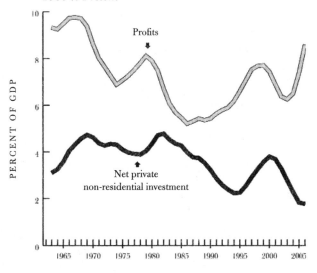

Sources: Bureau of Economic Analysis, National Income and Product Accounts, "Gross and Net Domestic Investment by Major Type, Annual Data 1929-2006," Table 5.2.5; *Economic Report of the President, 2008*, Tables B-1 (GDP) and Table B-91 (Domestic Industry Profits).

The fact that U.S. consumption (facilitated by the enormous U.S. current account deficit) has provided crucial effective demand for the production of other countries means that the slowdown in the United States
is already having disastrous effects abroad, with financial liquidation now
in high gear globally. "Emerging" and underdeveloped economies are
caught in a bewildering set of problems. This includes falling exports,
declining commodity prices, and the repercussions of high levels of financialization on top of an unstable and highly exploitative economic base—
while being subjected to renewed imperial pressures from the center
states.

The center states are themselves in trouble. Iceland, which has been
compared to the canary in the coal mine, has experienced a complete
financial meltdown, requiring rescue from outside, and possibly a massive
raiding of the pension funds of the citizenry. For more than seventeen
years Iceland has had a right-wing government led by the ultra-conserva-
tive Independence Party in coalition with the centrist social democratic
parties. Under this leadership Iceland adopted neoliberal financialization
and speculation to the hilt and saw an excessive growth of its banking and
finance sectors with total assets of its banks growing from 96 percent of
its GDP at the end of 2000 to nine times its GDP in 2006. Now Icelandic
taxpayers, who were not responsible for these actions, are being asked to
carry the burden of the overseas speculative debts of their banks, resulting in a drastic decline in the standard of living.[38]

A POLITICAL ECONOMY

Economics in its classical stage, which encompassed the work of both
possessive individualists like Adam Smith, David Ricardo, Thomas
Malthus, and John Stuart Mill, and socialist thinkers such as Karl Marx,
was called *political* economy. The name was significant because it pointed to the class basis of the economy and the role of the state.[39] To be sure,
Adam Smith introduced the notion of the "invisible hand" of the market
in replacing the former visible hand of the monarch. But, the political-
class context of economics was nevertheless omnipresent for Smith and
all the other classical economists. In the 1820s, as Marx observed, there

were "splendid tournaments" between political economists representing different classes (and class fractions) of society.

However, from the 1830s and '40s on, as the working class arose as a force in society, and as the industrial bourgeoisie gained firm control of the state, displacing landed interests (most notably with the repeal of the Corn Laws), economics shifted from its previous questioning form to the "bad conscience and evil intent of the apologetics."[40] Increasingly the circular flow of economic life was reconceptualized as a process involving only individuals, consuming, producing, and profiting on the margin. The concept of class thus disappeared in economics, but was embraced by the rising field of sociology (in ways increasingly abstracted from fundamental economic relationships). The state also was said to have nothing directly to do with economics and was taken up by the new field of political science.[41] Economics was thus "purified" of all class and political elements, and increasingly presented as a "neutral" science, addressing universal/transhistorical principles of capital and market relations.

Having lost any meaningful roots in society, orthodox neoclassical economics, which presented itself as a single paradigm, became a discipline dominated by largely meaningless abstractions, mechanical models, formal methodologies, and mathematical language, divorced from historical developments. It was anything but a science of the real world; rather its chief importance lay in its role as a self-confirming ideology. Meanwhile, actual business proceeded along its own lines largely oblivious (sometimes intentionally so) of orthodox economic theories. The failure of received economics to learn the lessons of the Great Depression, i.e., the inherent flaws of a system of class-based accumulation in its monopoly stage, included a tendency to ignore the fact that the real problem lay in the real economy, rather than in the monetary-financial economy.

Nothing looks more myopic than Bernanke's quick dismissal of traditional theories of the Great Depression that traced the underlying causes to the buildup of overcapacity and weak demand—inviting a similar dismissal of such factors today. Like his mentor Milton Friedman, Bernanke has stood for the dominant, neoliberal economic view of the last few decades, with its insistence that by holding back "the rock that starts a

landslide" it was possible to prevent a financial avalanche of "major proportions" indefinitely.[42] That the state of the ground above was shifting,
and that this was due to real, time-related processes, was of no genuine
concern. Ironically, Bernanke, the academic expert on the Great
Depression, adopted what had been described by Ethan Harris, chief
U.S. economist for Barclays Capital, as a "see no evil, hear no evil, speak
no evil" policy with respect to asset bubbles.[43]

It is therefore the contrary view, emphasizing the socioeconomic
contradictions of the system, to which it is now necessary to turn. For
a time in response to the Great Depression of the 1930s, in the work of
John Maynard Keynes, and various other thinkers associated with the
Keynesian, institutionalist, and Marxist traditions—the most important of which was the Polish economist Michal Kalecki—there was
something of a revival of political-economic perspectives. But following the Second World War Keynesianism was increasingly reabsorbed
into the system. This occurred partly through what was called the
"neoclassical-Keynesian synthesis"—which, as Joan Robinson, one of
Keynes's younger colleagues claimed, had the effect of bastardizing
Keynes—and partly through the closely related growth of military
Keynesianism.[44] Eventually, monetarism emerged as the ruling
response to the stagflation crisis of the 1970s, along with the rise of
other conservative free-market ideologies, such as supply-side theory,
rational expectations, and the new classical economics (summed up as
neoliberal orthodoxy). Economics lost its explicit political-economic
cast, and the world was led back once again to the mythology of self-
regulating, self-equilibrating markets free of issues of class and power.
Anyone who questioned this, was characterized as *political* rather than
economic, and thus largely excluded from the mainstream economic
discussion.[45]

Needless to say, economics never ceased to be political; rather the pol-
itics that was promoted was so closely intertwined with the system of economic power as to be nearly invisible. Adam Smith's visible hand of the
monarch had been transformed into the invisible hand, not of the market,
but of the capitalist class, which was concealed behind the veil of the mar-

ket and competition. Yet, with every major economic crisis that veil has been partly torn aside and the reality of class power exposed.

Secretary of the Treasury Paulson's request to Congress in September 2008 for $700 billion with which to bail out the financial system may constitute a turning point in the popular recognition of, and outrage over, the economic problem, raising for the first time in many years the issue of a *political* economy. It immediately became apparent to the entire population that the critical question in the financial crisis and in the deep economic stagnation that was emerging was: *Who will pay?* The answer of the capitalist system, left to its own devices, was the same as always: the costs would be borne disproportionately by those at the bottom. The old game of privatization of profits and socialization of losses would be replayed for the umpteenth time. The population would be called upon to "tighten their belts" to "foot the bill" for the entire system. The capacity of the larger public to see through this deception in the months and years ahead will of course depend on an enormous amount of education by trade union and social movement activists, and the degree to which the empire of capital is stripped naked by the crisis.

There is no doubt that the present growing economic bankruptcy and political outrage have produced a fundamental break in the continuity of the historical process. How should progressive forces approach this crisis? First of all, it is important to discount any attempts to present the serious economic problems that now face us as a kind of "natural disaster." They have a cause, and it lies in the system itself. And although those at the top of the economy certainly did not welcome the crisis, they nonetheless have been the main beneficiaries of the system, shamelessly enriching themselves at the expense of the rest of the population, and should be held responsible for the main burdens now imposed on society. It is the well-to-do who should foot the bill—not only for reasons of elementary justice, but also because they collectively and *their system* constitute the reason that things are as bad as they are; and because the best way to help both the economy and those at the bottom is to address the needs of the latter directly. There should be no golden parachutes for the capitalist class paid for at taxpayer expense.

But capitalism takes advantage of social inertia, using its power to rob outright when it can't simply rely on "normal" exploitation. Without a revolt from below the burden will simply be imposed on those at the bottom. All of this requires a mass social and economic upsurge, such as in the latter half of the 1930s, including the revival of unions and mass social movements of all kinds—using the power for change granted to the people in the Constitution; even going so far as to threaten the current duopoly of the two-party system.

What should such a radical movement from below, if it were to emerge, seek to do under these circumstances? Here we hesitate to say, not because there is any lack of needed actions to take, but because a radicalized political movement determined to sweep away decades of exploitation, waste, and irrationality will, if it surfaces, be like a raging storm, opening whole new vistas for change. Anything we suggest at this point runs the double risk of appearing far too radical now and far too timid later on.

Some liberal economists and commentators argue that, given the present economic crisis, nothing short of a major public works program aimed at promoting employment, a kind of new New Deal, will do. Robert Kuttner has argued in *Obama's Challenge* that "an economic recovery will require more like $700 billion a year in new public outlay, or $600 billion counting offsetting cuts in military spending. Why? Because there is no other plausible strategy for both achieving a general economic recovery and restoring balance to the economy."[46] This, however, will be more difficult than it sounds. There are reasons to believe that the dominant economic interests would block an increase in civilian government spending on such a scale, even in a crisis, as interfering with the private market. The truth is that civilian government purchases were at 13.3 percent of GNP in 1939—what Baran and Sweezy in 1966 theorized as approximating their "outer limits"—and they have barely budged since then, with civilian government consumption and investment expenditures from 1960 to the present averaging 13.7 percent of GNP (13.8 percent of GDP).[47] The class forces blocking a major increase in nondefense governmental spending even in a severe stagnation should therefore not be underestimated. Any major advances in this direction will require a massive class struggle.

Still, there can be no doubt that change should be directed first and foremost to meeting the basic needs of people for food, housing, employment, health, education, a sustainable environment, etc. Will the government assume the responsibility for providing useful work to all those who desire and need it? Will housing be made available (free from crushing mortgages) to everyone, extending as well to the homeless and the poorly housed? Will a single-payer national health system be introduced to cover the needs of the entire population, replacing the worst and most expensive health care system in the advanced capitalist world? Will military spending be cut back drastically, dispensing with global imperial domination? Will the rich be heavily taxed and income and wealth be redistributed? Will the environment, both global and local, be protected? Will the right to organize be made a reality?

If such elementary prerequisites of any decent future look impossible under the present system, then the people should take it into their own hands to create a new society that will deliver these genuine *goods*. Above all it is necessary "to insist that morality and economics alike support the intuitive sense of the masses that society's human and natural resources can and should be used for all the people and not for a privileged minority."[48]

In the 1930s Keynes decried the growing dominance of financial capital, which threatened to reduce the real economy to "a bubble on a whirlpool of speculation," and recommended the "euthanasia of the rentier." However, financialization is so essential to the monopoly-finance capital of today, that such a "euthanasia of the rentier" cannot be achieved—in contravention of Keynes's dream of a more rational capitalism—without moving beyond the system itself. In this sense we are clearly at a global turning point, where the world will perhaps finally be ready to take the step, as Keynes also envisioned, of repudiating an alienated moral code of "fair is foul and foul is fair"—used to justify the greed and exploitation necessary for the accumulation of capital—turning it inside-out to create a more rational social order.[49] To do this, though, it is necessary for the population to seize control of their *political* economy, replacing the present system of capitalism with something amounting to a real political and economic democracy; what the present rulers of the world fear and decry most—as "socialism."[50]

Notes

PREFACE

1. "Recession-Plagued Nation Demands New Bubble to Invest In," *The Onion*, July 14, 2008, http://www.theoninon.com.

2. James Petras, "The Great Financial Crisis," August 25–26, 2007, http://www.counterpunch.com; "Who's to Blame for the Great Financial Crisis?," *Telegraph* (London), August 18, 2008, http://www.telegraph.co.uk.

INTRODUCTION

1. Joseph A. Schumpeter, *Business Cycles*, vol. 2 (New York: McGraw-Hill, 199), 1045.

2. Paul Krugman, "Desperately Seeking Seriousness," *New York Times*, October 26, 2008.

3. "Greenspan Testimony on Sources of Financial Crisis," *Wall Street Journal*, October 23, 2008.

4. John Kenneth Galbraith, *The Age of Uncertainty* (Boston: Houghton Mifflin, 1977), 216.

5. Alvin H. Hansen, *Full Recovery or Stagnation?* (New York: W. W. Norton, 1938); also Hansen, *Fiscal Policy and Business Cycles* (New York: W.W. Norton, 1941).

6. John Maynard Keynes, *The General Theory of Employment, Interest and Money* (London: Macmillan, 1973).

7. Alvin H. Hansen, "The Stagnation Thesis," in American Economic Association, *Readings in Fiscal Policy* (Homewood, Illinois: Richard D. Irwin, 1955), 540–57; Schumpeter, *Business Cycles*, vol. 2, 1033–50. See also John Bellamy Foster, "Investment and Capitalist Maturity," in Foster and Henryk Szlajfer, ed., *The Faltering Economy* (New York: Monthly Review Press, 1984),

142   NOTES TO PAGES 14-19

57–73, and "What Is Stagnation?," in Robert Cherry et al., *The Irreversible Crisis* (New York: Union for Radical Political Economics, 1987), 59–70.

8.   Michal Kalecki, *Theory of Economic Dynamics* (London: George Allen and Unwin, 1954), 161.

9.   Joan Robinson, "Review of *Money, Trade and Economic Growth* by J. G. Johnson," *Economic Journal* 72, no. 287 (September 1962): 690–92; Lynn Turgeon, *Bastard Keynesianism* (Westport, Conn.: Greenwood Press, 1996).

10. Paul Samuelson, *Economics: An Introductory Analysis* (New York: McGraw Hill, 1964), 730.

11. Paul A. Baran and Paul M. Sweezy, *Monopoly Capital: An Essay on the American Economic and Social Order* (New York: Monthly Review Press, 1966), 108. Baran and Sweezy were strongly influenced by Kalecki and by Josef Steindl's *Maturity and Stagnation in American Capitalism* (Oxford: Basil Blackwell, 1952).

12. As Galbraith once observed, "Under-consumption and underinvestment are the same side of the same coin." John Kenneth Galbraith, *The Great Crash* (Boston: Houghton Mifflin, 1979), 156.

13. Baran and Sweezy also considered, primarily under the influence of Schumpeter, the question of whether a new epoch-making innovation on the scale of the steam engine, railroad, and the automobile, greatly expanding the demand for capital, might enter in to pull the system out of stagnation. Although they considered this a possibility, all that could be said was that no such epoch-making innovation was then on the horizon. See Baran and Sweezy, *Monopoly Capital*, 219–22.

14. Joan Robinson, *Essays in the Theory of Economic Fluctuations* (London: Macmillan, 1962), 53–54; *Contributions to Modern Economics* (Oxford: Basil Blackwell, 1978), 213.

15. Robert Pollin, *Contours of Descent* (New York: Verso, 2003), 14–16.

16. John Maynard Keynes, *Essays in Persuasion* (New York: Harcourt, Brace, and Co., 1932), 169.

17. Keynes, *The General Theory*, 159.

18. Hyman P. Minsky, "Hyman P. Minsky (1919–1996)" (autobiographical article originally written in 1992), in Philip Arestis and Malcolm Sawyer, *A Biographical Dictionary of Dissenting Economists* (Northampton, Massachusetts: Edward Elgar, 2000), 411–16. See also Hyman P. Minsky, *Stabilizing an Unstable Economy* (New Haven: Yale University Press, 1986). Minsky's ideas were given greater currency through the work of Charles P. Kindleberger in his *Manias, Panics, and Crashes: A History of Financial Crises* (Hoboken, New Jersey: John Wiley and Sons, 1978).

19. Paul M. Sweezy and Harry Magdoff, *The Dynamics of U.S. Capitalism* (New York: Monthly Review Press, 1972), 7–29.

20. "The Casino Society," *Business Week*, September 16, 1985; Magdoff and Sweezy, *Stagnation and the Financial Explosion*, 143.

21. See, for example, James Crotty, "The Neoliberal Paradox," in *Financialization and the World Economy*, ed. Gerald A. Epstein (Northampton, Massachusetts: Edward Elgar, 2005), 77–110.

22. Karl Marx, *Capital*, vol. 3 (New York: International Publishers), 250, 259 (chapter 15, sections 2-3). The fact that capitalism in the late nineteenth century was already increasingly prone to stagnation was pointed out a number of times by Frederick Engels who wrote of "stagnation [that] lasts for years; productive forces and products are wasted and destroyed wholesale, until the accumulated mass of commodities finally filter off, more or less depreciated in value, until production and exchange gradually begin to move again [which] . . . after breakneck leaps, ends where it began in the ditch of a crisis." Engels, *Socialism: Utopian and Scientific* (New York: International Publishers, 1978), 64.

23. The one notable exception to this is on the first page of chapter 5, where in order to avoid repetition in the book we eliminated a long quote and replaced it with straight discussion, with no substantive change in the argument.

24. We have, however, addressed this elsewhere as in John Bellamy Foster, Harry Magdoff, and Robert W. McChesney (with the assistance of Fred Magdoff), "What Recovery?," *Monthly Review* 54, no. 11 (April 2003): 8–11.

25. The issue of a "new New Deal" was discussed by Magdoff and Sweezy in the late 1980s. See their "A New New Deal," *Monthly Review*, 43, no. 9 (February 1982), 1–10.

26. John Kenneth Galbraith, *The Economics of Innocent Fraud* (Boston: Houghton Mifflin, 2004), 60.

27. John Bellamy Foster, Hannah Holleman, and Robert W. McChesney, "The U.S. Imperial Triangle and Military Spending," *Monthly Review*, 60, no. 5 (October 2008): 1–19; John Bellamy Foster, *Naked Imperialism* (New York: Monthly Review Press, 2006).

CHAPTER 1: THE HOUSEHOLD DEBT BUBBLE

1. See U.S. Department of Labor, Bureau of Labor Statistics, *Consumer Expenditures in 2003*, June 2005, Table 1, http://www.bls.gov/cex/.

2. Clark quoted in Paul M. Sweezy, *The Theory of Capitalist Development* (New York: Monthly Review Press, 1970), 168–69.

3. "Economy Up, People Down," August 31, 2005, and "Real Compensation Down as Wage Squeeze Continues," January 31, 2006, Economic Policy Institute, http://www.epi.org.

4. The shares of investment, government, and exports remained the same in 1994 and 2004 at 16, 19, and 10 percent, respectively, while the share of imports (subtracted from GDP) went from –12 to –15 percent. U.S. Department of Labor, Bureau of Labor Statistics, *Occupational Outlook Quarterly* 49, no. 4 (Winter 2005-06): 42, http://www.bls.gov/opub/ooq/2005/winter/contents.htm.

5. In the Survey of Consumer Finances "family" has a meaning close to that of

household (encompassing even single individual households under the term "family"). Hence, the two terms are used interchangeably in the present article. As stated in the Federal Reserve Bulletin article presenting the results of the survey: "The definition of 'family' used throughout this article differs from that typically used in other government studies. In the SCF, a household unit is divided into a 'primary economic unit' (PEU)—the family—and everyone else in the household. The PEU is intended to be the economically dominant single individual or couple (whether married or living together as partners) and all other persons in the household who are financially interdependent with that economically dependent person or household" (A36).

6. Kevin Phillips, *American Theocracy* (New York: Viking, 2006), 324–25.

7. "Recent Changes in U.S. Family Finances" (see note to Table 2 in this article), A28–A29.

8. "Household Financial Indicators," Board of Governors, Federal Reserve System, *Flow of Funds*, 2006.

9. Doug Henwood, "Leaking Bubble," *The Nation*, March 27, 2006.

10. "The Credit-Cart Catapult," *Wall Street Journal*, March 25, 2006; Phillips, *American Theocracy*, 327.

11. "Recent Changes in U.S. Family Finances" (see note to Table 2), A28.

12. The Center for Responsible Lending and the Consumer Federation of America, *Car Title Lending* (April 14, 2005), http://www.responsiblelending.org.

13. "As Debt Collectors Multiply, So Do Consumer Complaints," *Washington Post*, July 28, 2005.

14. "Household Financial Conditions: Q4 2005," Financial Markets Center, March 19, 2006, http://www.fmcenter.org.

15. Stephanie Pomboy, "The Great Bubble Transfer," MacroMavens, April 3, 2002, http://www.macromavens.com/reports/the_great_bubble_transfer.pdf.

16. See for example the treatment of this in Council of Economic Advisors, *The Economic Report of the President, 2006*, 29–30, http://www.gpoaccess.gov/eop/.

17. Stephanie Pomboy, "Handling the Truth," *Barron's*, February 7, 2005, http://www.macromavens.com/reports/barron's_interview.pdf; "Wal-Mart Fishes Upstream," *Business Week* Online, March 24, 2006.

18. Pomboy, "Handling the Truth"; "Too Much Cash," *Barron's*, November 7, 2005. See also "Long on Cash, Short on Ideas," *New York Times*, December 5, 2004.

CHAPTER 2: THE EXPLOSION OF DEBT AND SPECULATION

1. Paul M. Sweezy and Harry Magdoff, The *Dynamics of U.S. Capitalism* (New York: Monthly Review Press, 1972); Harry Magdoff and Paul M. Sweezy, *The End of Prosperity* (New York: Monthly Review Press, 1977), *The Deepening Crisis of U.S. Capitalism* (New York: Monthly Review Press, 1981), *Stagnation and the Financial Explosion* (New York: Monthly Review Press, 1987), and *The Irreversible Crisis* (New York: Monthly Review Press, 1988).

2. Karl Marx, *Capital*, vol. 3 (New York: International Publishers, 1967), 507 (chapter 32).

3.   See Stephanie Aaronson et al., "The Recent Decline in Labor Force Participation Rate and Its Implications for Potential Labor Supply," *Brookings Papers on Economic Activity*, no.1 (2006): 69-134.

4.   "The Odd Recovery: Unemployment Is Low and So is Employment," *New York Times*, September 2, 2006.

5.   Magdoff and Sweezy, *Stagnation and the Financial Explosion* (New York: Monthly Review Press, 1987), 24.

6.   Calculated from *Economic Report of the President, 2006*, Table B-91.

7.   Harry Magdoff, "A Letter to a Contributor: The Same Old State," *Monthly Review* 49, no. 8 (January 1998): 5.

8.   Calculated from National Income and Product Accounts, Table 1.1.5.

9.   The data on military expenditures is from official figures, and thus excludes much of what should be included in military spending, e.g., homeland security, much of NASA, parts of the State Department budget, veterans' benefits, etc. For a classic treatment of this problem see James Cypher, "The Basic Economics of 'Rearming America,'" *Monthly Review 33*, no. 6 (November 1981): 11-27.

10.   When the amount of government debt is used, as in total U.S. debt, this includes debt held by federal agencies, such as the Social Security Administration. The amount of this debt is currently $3 trillion—representing close to 42 percent of the total federal debt. Although technically it is a debt owed by the government to itself, in reality it is a debt to particular people—for example, those that will be retired on Social Security when there is less Social Security tax coming in than needed to pay retirees.

11.   Gregory Zuckerman, "Companies on a Borrowing Binge: Can They Handle All the Debt?" *Wall Street Journal*, August 17, 2006.

12.   "As Economy Thrived Under Greenspan, So Did Debt," *Washington Post*, January 23, 2006.

13.   "Homeowners Start to Feel the Pain of Rising Rates," *Wall Street Journal*, August 10, 2006.

14.   Bureau of Economic Analysis release 0634, August 1, 2006.

15.   Federal Reserve Flow of Funds.

16.   "Homeowners Start to Feel the Pain of Rising Rates," *Wall Street Journal*, August 10, 2006.

17.   "Nightmare Mortgages," *Business Week*, September 11, 2006.

18.   "IMF Warns Lingering Imbalances May Spur Volatile Fall in Dollar," *Wall Street Journal*, September 13, 2006.

19.   "Warning from the Markets," *New York Times*, February 24, 2005.

20.   "Ahead of the Tape," *Wall Street Journal*, March 7, 2006.

21.   Harry Magdoff and Paul M. Sweezy, "Production and Finance," *Monthly Review*, 35, no. 1, (May 1983), 1-13.

22.   "Corporate America's New Achilles' Heel," *Business Week*, March 28, 2005.

23.   Ibid.

24.   "Din of Roaring Corporate-Debt Market Drowns Out Growing Talk of a

Bubble," *Wall Street Journal*, March 3, 2006.

25. http://www.nyse.com.
26. Craig Karmin and Michael R. Sesit, "Currency Markets Draw Speculation, Fraud," *Wall Street Journal*, July 26, 2005.
27. "Back of the Envelope," *New York Times*, September 22, 2006.
28. "A Hedge Fund's Loss Rattles Nerves," *New York Times*, September 19, 2006.
29. "Smokin' LBOs," November 18, 2005, http://wwwforbes.com/2005/11/17/lbo-buyouts-banks-lonas-cx_lm_1118lob.html.
30. "Blizzard of Deals Heralds an Era of Megamergers," *Wall Street Journal*, June 27, 2006.
31. "Capital Pains: Big Cash Hoards," *Wall Street Journal*, July 21, 2006.
32. "Buy It, Strip It, Then Flip It," *Business Week*, August 7, 2006, 28–31.
33. "Private Money: The New Financial Order," *Wall Street Journal*, July 25, 2006.
34. "Huge Buyout of Hospital Group Highlights Era of Going Private," *New York Times*, July 25, 2006.
35. "Private Money: The New Financial Order," *Wall Street Journal*, July 25, 2006.
36. "Big Debt Often Lurks Behind IPOs," *Wall Street Journal*, May 15, 2006.
37. For example, see "The Dark Side of Debt," *The Economist*, September 23, 2006.
38. "Hedge Funds and Derivatives and Their Implications for the Financial System" (speech, Federal Reserve Bank of New York, September 15, 2006), available at http://www.newyorkfed.org/newsevents/speeches/2006/gei060914.html.

CHAPTER 3: MONOPOLY-FINANCE CAPITAL

1. Paul M. Sweezy, "The Triumph of Financial Capital," *Monthly Review* 46, no 2 (June 1994): 1–11.
2. In using the term "finance capital" here we are not doing so in the specific sense in which it was introduced in Rudolf Hilferding's great work *Finance Capital* (1910) where it was defined at one point as "capital controlled by the banks and utilized by the industrialists." Rather the term is meant in this case to refer to the employment of money capital in financial markets and speculation more generally. In this regard, Doug Henwood's sharp criticism of Hilferding's position on bank control is worth quoting: "I'm very critical of Hilferding ... for arguing that the German-style model of capitalism, with a handful of big banks owning big industrial concerns, was the future of the system, and that the Anglo-American stock-market system was on the way out. He couldn't have been more wrong; as the gloomy Wall Street economist Henry Kaufman put it a few years ago, we're seeing the Americanization of global finance." Doug Henwood interviewed by Geert Lovink, "Finance and Economics after the Dotcom Crash," December 20, 2001, http://www.nettime.org. See also Paul M. Sweezy, *The Theory of Capitalist Development* (New York: Monthly Review Press, 1942), 266.
3. Joseph Schumpeter, *Capitalism, Socialism and Democracy* (New York: HarperCollins, 1942), 90n.

4.   Michal Kalecki, *Theory of Economic Dynamics* (London: George Allen and
      Unwin, 1954), 161. See also Josef Steindl, *Maturity and Stagnation in
      American Capitalism* (New York: Monthly Review Press, 1976).

5.   Later in their book Baran and Sweezy also pointed to historical factors, such as
      the second wave of automobilization of the U.S. economy in the 1950s (which
      included the building of the interstate highway system, the growth of the sub-
      urbs, etc.). However, the automobilization of the U.S. economy, they argued,
      was no longer an expansive factor, and was entering a period of simple repro-
      duction.

6.   *Paul M. Sweezy, "Monopoly Capital After Twenty-Five Years," Monthly Review*
      43, no. 7 (December 1991): 52–57.

7.   Paul M. Sweezy and Paul Baran, *Monopoly Capital: An Essay on the American
      Economic and Social Order* (New York: Monthly Review Press, 1966), 108. For
      a work applying this theory to today's global economy see Bill Lucarelli,
      Monopoly Capitalism in Crisis (New York: Palgrave Macmillan, 2004).

8.   The dominance of finance is not the same thing as a shift in power from non-
      financial to financial institutions, since the distinction between the two has
      become increasingly blurred. Non-financial corporations from General Motors
      to Wal-Mart are increasingly involved in lending activities from which they
      derive much of their income, as well as in outright speculative finance. For
      empirical evidence of what could be called the financialization of non-financial
      firms see Greta R. Krippner, "The Financialization of the American Economy,"
      Socio-Economic Review 3, no. 2 (2005): 173–208.

9.   Harry Magdoff and Paul M. Sweezy, "The Strange Recovery of 1983–84,"
      Monthly Review 37, no. 5 (October 1985): 1-11.

10.   *Monopoly Capital,* 139–41.

11.   Harry Magdoff, "Monopoly Capital," *Economic Development and Cultural
      Change* 16, no. 1 (October 1967): 145–50, and "Problems of United States
      Capitalism" in Paul M. Sweezy and Harry Magdoff, *The Dynamics of U.S.
      Capitalism* (New York: Monthly Review Press, 1972), 7–29.

12.   See in particular Harry Magdoff and Paul M. Sweezy, *Stagnation and the
      Financial Explosion* (New York: Monthly Review Press, 1987).

13.   See chapter 2. The figures on the debt explosion in the U.S. economy, though
      startling, underestimate the growth of financial speculation. There is no accept-
      ed way of measuring the full scale of such speculation since numerous financial
      instruments now exist that, as Henwood points out, are "completely outside the
      conceptual realm of traditional accounting, which can think of debt and equity,
      liabilities and assets, but not more insubstantial instruments like options,
      futures, and inverse floaters. And unlike stocks or loans, it's hard to put a dol-
      lar volume on them, since the purported value of the transaction—the notional
      principal—is usually far more than the sum of money actually at risk....But the
      very immeasurability of the things underscores the point about financialization:
      layers of claims have been piled upon layers of claims, most of them furiously
      traded, with some resisting definition and measurement...[I]f there were some

way to capture their growth, the line on the chart would no doubt run off the page." Doug Henwood, *After the New Economy* (New York: The New Press, 2005), 192. See also Doug Henwood, *Wall Street* (New York: Verso, 1997).

14. The enormous difficulties that economists encounter in any attempt to relate "real" and financial markets can be seen in John H. Cochrane, ed., *Financial Markets and the Real Economy* (Northampton, MA: Edward Elgar, 2006).

15. John Maynard Keynes, *The General Theory of Employment, Interest and Money* (London: Macmillan, 1973), 160–61.

16. Harry Magdoff and Paul M. Sweezy, "Production and Finance," *Monthly Review* 35, no. 1 (May 1983): 1–13.

17. John Maynard Keynes, *Essays in Persuasion* (New York: Harcourt, Brace and Co., 1932), 169.

18. Keynes, *The General Theory*, 159.

19. See chapter 2.

20. Hyman P. Minsky, *John Maynard Keynes* (New York: Columbia University Press, 1975), and *Can "It" Happen Again?: Essays on Instability and Finance* (Armonk, NY: M.E. Sharpe, 1982). See also Gary Dymski and Robert Pollin, eds., *New Perspectives in Monetary Macroeconomics: Explorations in the Tradition of Hyman P. Minsky* (Ann Arbor: University of Michigan Press, 1994).

21. Eric J. Weiner, *What Goes Up: The Uncensored History of Modern Wall Street* (New York: Little, Brown and Co., 2005).

22. Henwood, *After the New Economy*, 231.

23. "Housing Cools Down Economy," *New York Times*, October 28, 2006.

24. Michael M. Hutchinson and Frank Westermann, eds., *Japan's Great Stagnation* (Cambridge, MA: MIT Press, 2006).

25. *Business Week*, September 16, 1985.

26. Karl Marx, *Capital*, vol. 1 (London: Penguin, 1976), 799.

27. See The Editors, "A Prizefighter for Capitalism: Paul Krugman vs. the Quebec Protesters," *Monthly Review* 53, no. 2 (June 2001): 1–5.

CHAPTER 4: THE FINANCIALIZATION OF CAPITALISM

1. Gerald A. Epstein, "Introduction," in *Financialization and the World Economy*, ed. Gerald A. Epstein (Northampton, MA: Edward Elgar, 2005), 1.

2. See chapter 3.

3. The current usage of the term "financialization" owes much to the work of Kevin Phillips, who employed it in his *Boiling Point* (New York: Random House, 1993) and a year later devoted a key chapter of his *Arrogant Capital* to the "Financialization of America," defining financialization as "a *prolonged* split between the divergent real and financial economies" (New York: Little, Brown, and Co., 1994), 82. In the same year Giovanni Arrighi used the concept in an analysis of international hegemonic transition in *The Long Twentieth Century* (New York: Verso, 1994).

4. Harry Magdoff first raised the issue of a growing reliance on debt in the U.S.

economy in an article originally published in the *Socialist Register* in 1965. See Harry Magdoff and Paul M. Sweezy, *The Dynamics of U.S. Capitalism* (New York: Monthly Review Press, 1972), 13–16.

5. Robert Pollin, "Remembering Paul Sweezy: 'He Was an Amazingly Great Man,'" *Counterpunch*, http://www.counterpunch.org, March 6–7, 2004; "The Man Who Explained Empire: Remembering Harry Magdoff," *Counterpunch*, http://www.counterpunch.org, January 6, 2006.

6. Paul M. Sweezy, "More (or Less) on Globalization," *Monthly Review* 49, no. 4 (September 1997): 3–4.

7. Paul A. Baran and Paul M. Sweezy, *Monopoly Capital* (New York: Monthly Review Press, 1966).

8. James Tobin, "On the Efficiency of the Financial System," *Lloyd's Bank Review*, no. 153 (1984), 14–15.

9. In the following analysis I follow a long-standing economic convention in using the term "real economy" to refer to the realm of production (i.e. economic output as measured by GDP), as opposed to the financial economy. Yet both the "real economy" and the financial economy are obviously real in the usual sense of the word.

10. Harry Magdoff and Paul M. Sweezy, *Stagnation and the Financial Explosion* (New York: Monthly Review Press, 1987), 149. Magdoff and Sweezy were replying to an editorial in *Business Week* concluding its special September 16, 1985, issue on "The Casino Society."

11. Paul M. Sweezy, "Economic Reminiscences," *Monthly Review* 47, no. 1 (May 1995): 8; Lukas Menkhoff and Norbert Tolksdorf, *Financial Market Drift* (New York: Springer-Verlag, 2001).

12. The failure of investment banking to regain its position of power at the very apex of the system (as the so-called "money trust") that it had attained in the formative period of monopoly capitalism can be attributed to the fact that the conditions on which its power had rested in that period were transitory. See Paul M. Sweezy, "Investment Banking Revisited," *Monthly Review* 33, no. 10 (March 1982).

13. Harry Magdoff and Paul M. Sweezy, *The End of Prosperity* (New York: Monthly Review Press, 1977), 35.

14. Sweezy, "Economic Reminiscences," 8–9.

15. This is in line with the financial instability hypothesis of Keynes and Hyman Minsky. See Minsky, *Can "It" Happen Again?* (Armonk, New York: M. E. Sharpe, 1982).

16. Robert W. Parenteau, "The Late 1990s' US Bubble," in Epstein, ed., *Financialization and the World Economy*, 136–38.

17. Doug Henwood, *After the New Economy* (New York: The New Press, 2005), 231; Epstein, "Introduction," 4; Garry J. Schinasi, *Safeguarding Financial Stability* (Washington, D.C.: International Monetary Fund, 2006), 228–32. See also chapter 2 above.

18. Greta R. Krippner, "The Financialization of the American Economy," *Socio-*

economic Review 3, no. 2 (2005), 173–208; James Crotty, "The Neoliberal Paradox," in Epstein, ed., *Financialization and the World Economy*, 77–110.

19. Edward N. Wolff, "Changes in Household Wealth in the 1980s and 1990s in the U.S.," The Levy Economics Institute of Bard College, Working Paper No. 407 (May 2004), table 2, http://www.levy.org.

20. *New York Times*, March 1, 2007.

21. Pollin, "The Man Who Explained Empire."

22. *New York Times*, February 16, 2007.

23. *Le Monde Diplomatique*, December 1997.

24. See Daniela Magalhães Pates and Leda Maria Paulani, "The Financial Globalization of Brazil under Lula," and Fabríco Augusto de Loiveira and Paulo Nakatini, "The Brazilian Economy Under Lula," in *Monthly Review* 58, no. 9 (February 2007), 32–49.

25. International Monetary Fund, *The Global Financial Stability Report* (March 2003), 1–3, and (September 2006), 74–75.

26. Gabriel Kolko, "Why a Global Economic Deluge Looms," *Counterpunch*, http://www.counterpunch.org, June 15, 2006.

CHAPTER 5: THE FINANCIALIZATION OF CAPITAL AND THE CRISIS

1. Karl Marx, *Capital*, vol. 3 (New York: International Publishers, 1967), chapter 15, 250. To avoid repetition in the book format, a long indented quote included in the original article has been removed at this point and a few additional lines of text substituted. The thrust of the argument remains the same.

2. "U.S. Recovery May Take Longer than Usual: Greenspan," *Reuters*, February 25, 2008.

3. Paul M. Sweezy, "More (or Less) on Globalization," *Monthly Review* 49, no. 4 (September 1997): 3.

4. Stephanie Pomboy, "The Great Bubble Transfer," MacroMavens, April 3, 2002, http://www.macromavens.com/reports/the_great_bubble_transfer.pdf.

5. The following discussion of the five phases of the housing bubble relies primarily on the following sources: Juan Landa, "Deconstructing the Credit Bubble," *Matterhorn Capital Management Investor Update*, 3rd Quarter 2007, http://www.matterhorncap.com/pdf/3q2007.pdf, and "Subprime Collapse Part of Economic Cycle," *San Antonio Business Journal*, October 26, 2007, and Charles P. Kindleberger and Robert Aliber, *Manias, Panics, and Crashes* (Hoboken, New Jersey: John Wiley and Sons, 2005).

6. In the analysis of financial bubbles that Charles Kindleberger provided based on the earlier theory of financial instability introduced by Hyman Minsky, the phase in the bubble associated here with a "novel offering" is more frequently referred to as "displacement," a concept that is supposed to combine the ideas of economic shock and innovation. Since "novel offering" is, however, more descriptive of what actually happens in the formation of a bubble, it is often substituted for "displacement" in concrete treatments. See Kindleberger and

Aliber, *Manias, Panics, and Crashes*, 47–50.

7.   Floyd Norris, "Who's Going to Take the Financial Weight?," *New York Times*, October 26, 2007; "Default Fears Unnerve Markets," *Wall Street Journal*, January 18, 2008.

8.   Federal Reserve Bank of New York, "Historical Changes of the Target Federal Funds and Discount Rates," http://www.newyorkfed.org/markets/statistics/dlyrates/fedrate.html.

9.   Landa, "Deconstructing the Credit Bubble."

10.   Hyman Minsky, *Can "It" Happen Again?* (New York: M. E. Sharpe, 1982), 28–29.

11.   "Household Financial Condition: Q4 2005," Financial Markets Center, March 19, 2006, http://www.fmcenter.org.

12.   "Global Derivatives Market Expands to $516 Trillion (Update)," Bloomberg.com, November 22, 2007.

13.   "Bond Insurer Woes May Mean End of Loophole," *Reuters*, February 13, 2008.

14.   "Global Recession Risk Grows as U.S. 'Damage' Spreads," Bloomberg.com, January 28, 2008. This report refers to the world recession level, as depicted by economists, as 3 percent or lower. But 2.5 percent is probably more accurate, i.e., more closely in line with recent world recessions and IMF views.

15.   Stephen Roach, "America's Inflated Asset Prices Must Fall," *Financial Times*, January 8, 2008.

16.   "Decline in Home Prices Accelerates," *Wall Street Journal*, February 27, 2008.

17.   Eric Janszen, "The Next Bubble," *Harper's* (February 2008), 39–45.

18.   Roach, "America's Inflated Asset Prices Must Fall," and "You Can Almost Hear it Pop," *New York Times*, December 16, 2007.

19.   See chapter 2.

20.   The term "stagnation thesis" was originally associated primarily with Alvin Hansen's argument in response to the Great Depression. See Hansen, "The Stagnation Thesis" in American Economic Association, *Readings in Fiscal Policy* (Homewood, Illinois: Richard D. Irwin, Inc., 1955), 540–57. It was later applied to Baran and Sweezy's *Monopoly Capital*. See Harry Magdoff, "Monopoly Capital" (review), *Economic Development and Cultural Change* 16, no. 1 (October 1967): 148.

21.   The concept of the "wealth effect" refers to the tendency for consumption to grow independently of income due to rising asset prices under financialization. The earliest known use of the term was in a January 27, 1975, article in *Business Week* entitled "How Sagging Stocks Depress the Economy." Alan Greenspan employed the concept of the "wealth effect" in 1980 to refer to the effect of the increase in the price of homes in stimulating consumption by home owners—Greenspan, "The Great Malaise," *Challenge* 23, no. 1 (March–April 1980): 38. He later used it to rationalize the New Economy stock market bubble of the 1990s.

22.   Harry Magdoff and Paul M. Sweezy, "Production and Finance," *Monthly Review* 35, no. 1 (May 1983): 11–12.

23.   The basic argument here was articulated in numerous publications by Paul

Baran, Paul Sweezy, and Harry Magdoff in the 1950s through 1990s.

24. Federal Reserve Statistical Release, G.17, "Industrial Production and Capacity Utilization," February 15, 2008, http://www.federalreserve.gov/releases/g17/Current/default.htm; John Bellamy Foster, "The Limits of U.S. Capitalism: Surplus Capacity and Capacity Surplus," in *The Faltering Economy*, eds. Foster and Henryk Szlajfer (New York: Monthly Review Press, 1984), 207.

25. Harold G. Vatter, "The Atrophy of Net Investment," in *The Inevitability of Government Spending* (New York: Columbia University Press, 1990), 7–8. Vatter notes that net investment as a share of net national product (NNP) dropped by half between the last quarter of the nineteenth century and the mid-twentieth century.

26. "Companies Are Piling Up Cash," *New York Times*, March 4, 2008. This piling up of cash has been the product of the last decade, with the average level of cash as a percent of total assets of corporations in the Standard & Poor's 500-stock index doubling between 1998 and 2004 (and the median ratio tripling).

27. Chalmers Johnson, "Why the US Has Really Gone Broke," *Le Monde Diplomatique* (English edition), February 2008. Johnson's $1 trillion figure for U.S. military spending is arrived at by adding the supplemental requests for the wars in Iraq and Afghanistan to the Department of Defense fiscal year 2008 budget (creating a grand total of $766 billion), and then adding to this the hidden military spending in the budgets for the Department of Energy, the Department of Homeland Security, Veterans Affairs, etc.

28. Paul M. Sweezy, "Economic Reminiscences," *Monthly Review* 47, no. 1 (May 1995), 8–9.

29. Thomas I. Palley, "Financialization: What It Is and Why It Matters," *Working Paper Series*, no. 153, Political Economy Research Institute, November 2007, 1, 3, 8, 11, 21, http://www.peri.umass.edu/Publication.236+M505d3f0bd8c.0.html.

30. See Kindleberger and Aliber, *Manias, Panics, and Crashes*, 126–35.

31. Özgür Orhangazi, "Financialization and Capital Accumulation in the Non-Financial Corporate Sector," *Working Paper Series*, no. 149, Political Economy Research Institute, October 2007, 3–7, 45, http://www.peri.umass.edu/Publication.236+M547c453b405.0.html.

32. Harry Magdoff and Paul M. Sweezy, *The Irreversible Crisis* (New York: Monthly Review Press, 1988), 49.

33. Sweezy, "Economic Reminiscences," 9–10.

CHAPTER 6: BACK TO THE REAL ECONOMY

1. Harry Magdoff and Paul M. Sweezy, *The Irreversible Crisis* (New York: Monthly Review Press, 1988), 76.

2. James K. Galbraith, *The Predator State* (New York: The Free Press, 2008), 48.

3. "Congressional Leaders Were Stunned by Warnings," *New York Times*, September 19, 2008.

4. Manas Chakravarty and Mobis Philipose, "Liquidity Trap: Fear of Failure,"

Livemint.com, October 11, 2008; John Maynard Keynes, *The General Theory of Employment, Interest and Money* (London: Macmillan, 1973), 174.

5. "Drama Behind a $250 Billion Banking Deal," *New York Times*, October 15, 2008.

6. "Government's Leap into Banking Has Its Perils," *New York Times*, October 18, 2008.

7. "Single-Family Homes in U.S. Fall to a 26-Year Low," Bloomberg.net, October 17, 2008; "Economic Fears Reignite Market Slump," *Wall Street Journal*, October 16, 2008.

8. See "Depression of 2008: Are We Heading Back to the 1930s?" *Times* (London), October 5, 2008. On the Japanese stagnation, see Paul Burkett and Martin Hart-Landsberg, "The Economic Crisis in Japan," *Critical Asian Studies* 35, no. 3 (2003): 339–72.

9. "The U.S. Is Said to Be Urging New Mergers in Banking," *New York Times*, October 21, 2008.

10. "CDO Cuts Show $1 Trillion Corporate-Debt Bets Toxic," Bloomberg.net, October 22, 2008.

11. "Banks Are Likely to Hold Tight to Bailout Money," *New York Times*, October 17, 2008.

12. Hyman Minsky, *Can "It" Happen Again?* (New York: M. E. Sharpe, 1982), vii–xxiv; "Hard Lessons to Be Learnt from a Minsky Moment," *Financial Times*, September 18, 2008. Riccardo Bellofiore and Joseph Halevi, "A Minsky Moment?: The Subprime Crisis and the New Capitalism," in C. Gnos and L. P. Rochon, *Credit, Money and Macroeconomic Policy: A Post-Keynesian Approach* (Cheltenham, forthcoming Edward Elgar). For Magdoff and Sweezy's views on Minsky see *The End of Prosperity* (New York: Monthly Review Press, 1977), 133–36.

13. Irving Fisher, "The Debt-Deflation Theory of Great Depressions," *Econometrica*, no. 4 (October 1933): 344; Paul Krugman, "The Power of De," *New York Times*, September 8, 2008.

14. "Amid Pressing Problems the Threat of Deflation Looms," *Wall Street Journal*, October 18, 2008; "A Monetary Malaise," *Economist*, October 11–17, 2008, 24.

15. Ben S. Bernanke, "Deflation: Making Sure 'It' Doesn't Happen Here," National Economists Club, Washington, D.C., November 21, 2002, http://www.federalreserve.gov.

16. Ethan S. Harris, *Ben Bernanke's Fed* (Cambridge, Massachusetts: Harvard University Press, 2008), 2, 173. Milton Friedman, *The Optimum Quantity of Money and Other Essays* (Chicago: Aldine Publishing, 1969), 4–14

17. Ben S. Bernanke, *Essays on the Great Depression* (Princeton: Princeton University Press, 2000), 5; Milton Friedman and Anna Schwartz, *A Monetary History of the United States, 1867–1960* (Princeton: Princeton University Press, 1963). For more realistic views of the Great Depression, taking into account the real economy, as well as monetary factors, and viewing it from the

standpoint of the stagnation of investment, which above all characterized the Depression, see Michael A. Bernstein, *The Great Depression* (Cambridge: Cambridge University Press, 1987), and Richard B. DuBoff, *Accumulation and Power* (New York: M.E. Sharpe, 1989), 84–92. On classic theories of the Great Depression see William A. Stoneman, *A History of the Economic Analysis of the Great Depression in America* (New York: Garland Publishing, 1979).

18. Ben S. Bernanke, "Money, Gold, and the Great Depression," H. Parker Willis Lecture in Economic Policy, Washington and Lee University, Lexington, Virginia, March 2, 2004, http://www.federalreserve.gov.

19. Ben S. Bernanke, "Some Thoughts on Monetary Policy in Japan," Japan Society of Monetary Economics, Tokyo, May 31, 2003, http://www.federalreserve.gov.

20. Bernanke, *Essays on the Great Depression*, 43.

21. "On Milton Friedman's Ninetieth Birthday," Conference to Honor Milton Friedman, University of Chicago, November 8, 2002, http://www.federalreserve.gov/BOARDOCS/SPEECHES/2002/20021108/default.htm. Ironically, Anna Schwartz, now 91, indicated in an interview for the *Wall Street Journal* that the Fed under Bernanke was fighting the last war, failing to perceive that the issue was uncertainty about solvency of the banks, not a question of liquidity as in the lead-up to the Great Depression. "Bernanke Is Fighting the Last War: Interview of Anna Schwartz," *Wall Street Journal*, October 18, 2008.

22. Ben S. Bernanke, "Asset Prices and Monetary Policy," speech to the New York Chapter of the National Association for Business Economics, New York, N.Y., October 15, 2002, http://www.federalreserve.gov; Harris, *Ben Bernanke's Fed*, 147–58.

23. Ben S. Bernanke, "The Economic Outlook," October 25, 2005, http://www.whitehouse.gov/cea/econ-outlook20051020.html; quoted in Robert Shiller, *The Subprime Option* (Princeton: Princeton University Press, 2008), 40.

24. Magdoff and Sweezy, *The Irreversible Crisis*, 76; Burkett and Hart-Landsberg, "The Economic Crisis in Japan," 347, 354–56, 36–66; Paul Krugman, "It's Baaack: Japan's Slump and the Return of the Liquidity Trap," *Brookings Papers on Economic Activity*, no. 2 (1998), 141–42, 174–78; Michael M. Hutchinson and Frank Westermann, eds., *Japan's Great Stagnation* (Cambridge, Massachusetts: MIT Press, 2006).

25. Magdoff and Sweezy, *The Irreversible Crisis*, 51.

26. Magdoff and Sweezy, *The End of Prosperity*, 136; Hyman Minsky, *John Maynard Keynes* (New York: Columbia University Press, 1975), 164.

27. Greenspan quoted, *New York Times*, October 9, 2008. See also John Bellamy Foster, Harry Magdoff, and Robert W. McChesney, "The New Economy: Myth and Reality," *Monthly Review* 52, no. 11 (April 2001), 1–15.

28. Manas Chakravarty, "A Turning Point in the Global Economic System," Livemint.com, September 17, 2008, http://www.livemint.com/2008/09

/17002644/A-turning-point-for-the-global.html.

29. See John Bellamy Foster, *Naked Imperialism* (New York: Monthly Review Press, 2006), 45-50.

30. Jim Reid, "A Trillion-Dollar Mean Reversion?," Deutsche Bank, July 15, 2008, http://www.nuclearphynance.com/User%20Files/85/thought_of_jim_14july.pdf.

31. See Paul A. Baran and Paul M. Sweezy, *Monopoly Capital* (New York: Monthly Review Press, 1966); Harry Magdoff and Paul M. Sweezy, *The Dynamics of U.S. Capitalism* (New York: Monthly Review Press, 1972), *The Deepening Crisis of U.S. Capitalism* (New York: Monthly Review Press, 1981), and *Stagnation and the Financial Explosion* (New York: Monthly Review Press, 1987).

32. Bellofiore and Halevi, "A Minsky Moment?"

33. See Michael Yates, *Longer Hours, Fewer Jobs* (New York: Monthly Review Press, 1994); Michael Perelman, *The Confiscation of American Prosperity* (New York: Palgrave Macmillan, 2007).

34. *Economic Report of the President, 2008*, Table B-47, 282.

35. Correspondents of the *New York Times*, *Class Matters* (New York: Times Books, 2005), 186; Edward N. Wolff, ed., *International Perspectives on Household Wealth* (Cheltenham: Edward Elgar, 2006), 112-15.

36. For a class breakdown of household debt see chapter 1 in this book.

37. Ben S. Bernanke, "The Global Savings Glut and the U.S. Current Account Deficit," Sandridge Lecture, Virginia Association of Economics, Richmond, Virginia, March 10, 2005, http://www.federalreserve.gov.

38. Steingrímur J. Stigfússon, "On the Financial Crisis of Iceland," *MRzine*.org, October 20, 2008; "Iceland in a Precarious Position," *New York Times*, October 8, 2008; "Iceland Scrambles for Cash," *Wall Street Journal*, October 6, 2008.

39. See Edward J. Nell, *Growth, Profits and Prosperity* (Cambridge: Cambridge University Press, 1980), 19-28.

40. Karl Marx, *Capital*, vol. 1 (New York: Vintage, 1976), 96-98.

41. See Crawford B. Macpherson, *Democratic Theory* (Oxford: Oxford University Press, 1973), 195-203.

42. Friedman and Schwartz, *A Monetary History of the United States*, 419.

43. Harris, *Ben Bernanke's Fed*, 147-58.

44. See John Bellamy Foster, Hannah Holleman, and Robert W. McChesney, "The U.S. Imperial Triangle and Military Spending," *Monthly Review* 60, no. 5 (October 2008): 1-19.

45. For a discussion of the simultaneous stagnation of the economy and of economics since the 1970s see Perelman, *The Confiscation of American Prosperity*. See also E. Ray Canterbery, *A Brief History of Economics* (River Edge, New Jersey: World Scientific Publishing, 2001), 417-26.

46. Robert Kuttner, *Obama's Challenge* (White River Junction, Vermont: Chelsea Green, 2008), 27.

47. Baran and Sweezy, *Monopoly Capital,* 159, 161; *Economic Report of the President, 2008,* 224, 250.

48. Harry Magdoff and Paul M. Sweezy, "The Crisis and the Responsibility of the Left," *Monthly Review* 39, no. 2 (June 1987): 1–5.

49. See Keynes, *The General Theory of Employment, Interest, and Money,* 376, and *Essays in Persuasion* (New York: Harcourt Brace and Co., 1932), 372; Paul M. Sweezy, "The Triumph of Financial Capital," *Monthly Review* 46, no. 2 (June 1994): 1–11; John Bellamy Foster, "The End of Rational Capitalism," *Monthly Review* 56, no. 10 (March 2005): 1–13.

50. In this respect, it is necessary, we believe, to go beyond liberal economics, and to strive for a ruthless critique of everything existing. Even a relatively progressive liberal economist, such as Paul Krugman, recent winner of the Bank of Sweden's prize for economics in honor of Alfred Nobel, makes it clear that what makes him a mainstream thinker, and hence a member of the club at the top of society, is his strong commitment to capitalism and "free markets" and his disdain of socialism—proudly proclaiming that "just a few years ago . . . one magazine even devoted a cover story to an attack on me for my pro-capitalist views"; Paul Krugman, *The Great Unraveling* (New York: W. W. Norton, 2004), xxxvi. In this context, see Harry Magdoff, John Bellamy Foster, and Robert W. McChesney, "A Prizefighter for Capitalism: Paul Krugman vs. the Quebec Protestors," *Monthly Review* 53, no. 2 (June 2001): 1–5.

INDEX

acquisitions, *see* mergers and acquisitions
adjustable rate mortgages, 33, 51, 96, 97
Amaranth Advisors (hedge fund), 58
Arrighi, Giovanni, 148*n*3
assassinations, 57
Asworth, Paul, 116
automobiles: invention of, as economic stimulus, 42; loans for, 34; manufacturers of, 113; in U.S. economy, 147*n*5

bankruptcies, 32, 51
banks, 45; cash hoarded by, 115, 120; collateralized debt obligations issued by, 94–95; failures of, 98; governments buying shares in, 113; loans made by, 54–55; mergers of, 114; overextension of debt of, 83
Baran, Paul A., 14–15; *Monopoly Capital* by, 63–72, 76, 79, 83, 126; on stagnation, 128, 142*n*11
Bear Stearns, 11, 98
Bellofiore, Riccardo, 129
Bernanke, Ben S., 85, 112, 117–20; on global savings glut, 132; on Great Depression, 135–36
Brazil, 87
Bretton Woods System, 87
bubbles (financial), 7, 16–17, 72; Bernanke on, 119; in housing, 35–36, 50–51, 73, 86, 91–92; in Japan, 106–7; phases of, 93–99; in stock market, 50
Burger King Corporation, 59
Bush, George W., 51

capital: Marx on accumulation of, 45, 54; Marx on overproduction of, 20
capitalism, 137–38; finance in, 15–16; financialization of, 77–81; investments needed for, 12–13; Krugman on, 156*n*50; Minsky on depressions tied to, 17; stagnation in, 39–40; stagnation and financialization in, 19; stagnation as normal state of, 14–15, 101, 128; transformation into monopoly-

finance capitalism, 64; *see also* monopoly-finance capital
capitalist class, 85
Carlyle, Thomas, 14
Chakravarty, Manas, 125–26
China, 73
Clark, J.B., 28
class, *see* social class
Clinton administration, 51
collateralized debt obligations (CDOs), 94–95, 97
collateralized-loan obligations (CLOs), 56, 94
Collateralized Mortgage Obligations (CMOs), 94
consumption: debts and increases in, 28–32; decline in, 113; expenditures on, 27; in global economy, 86; increase in, 131; tied to housing, 36; wealth effect and, 151*n*21; by working class, 37
corporations: borrowing by, 45; cash held by, 37, 53, 104, 152*n*26; debts of, 47–48; debts in earnings of, 54; distinction between non-financial and financial, 85, 147*n*8; mergers and acquisitions among, 58–60, 66–67; in transformation of capitalism into monopoly-finance capitalism, 64
credit: expansion of, 95–96; *see also* debts
credit card debts, 33–34
credit derivatives market, 84
currencies, 21, 52; derivative contracts in, 58; Tobin tax on international transactions in, 80; trading in, 56–57

Daschle, Tom, 57
debt collectors, 34–35
debts: bubbles and, 100; consumer, increase in, 28–32, 86; in corporate mergers and acquisitions, 60; credit card debts, 33–34; debt collectors, 34–35; expansion of, 45–52, 73, 121–22; on financial institutions, 54–56; financialization as growth in, 20; financial speculation and, 53; of government,